Grammar Four

Jennifer Seidl

Oxford University Press

Contents

1 Country life — Present simple; Adverbs of frequency; Present continuous

Sarah Davis **lives** in Dalton, Australia, where her parents **own** a sheep farm. Dalton **is** a small country town with a population of one hundred. The nearest city **is** over one hundred and fifty kilometres away, so Sarah **doesn't often go** there. She **likes** her life on the farm. She **has** a brother called Jeff. They both **go** to the local school. In summer it**'s usually** very hot, so the school day **starts** early at half past seven and **finishes** at midday.

At the moment Jack Davis **is working** in the wool-shed. It**'s** the sheep-shearing season and six men **are shearing** his sheep. He **is sorting** the good wool from the bad wool and **is putting** it into two piles. Sarah **is taking** the good wool to the wool-store. The work in the wool-shed **is** hard, but Sarah and Jeff **don't mind** because it**'s** good fun. The sheep-shearing **happens once a year**. Jeff **enjoys** working with the animals. When he **isn't helping** his father, he **reads** books about farming. He **is going** to university **next year** to study farming.

When they **finish** in the shed, Sarah and Jeff **are going** for a swim in the river. They **often go** to the river for a swim, and **sometimes visit** their old friend the platypus, who **lives** on the river bank.

sheep-shearing cutting the wool off the sheep

platypus

Grammar lesson

Present simple

Form

I/you/we/they **live**   he/she/it **lives**

The spelling sometimes changes.
  finish → it finish**es**
  go → he go**es**
  carry → she carr**ies**

We make questions with **do** or **does** + infinitive.
  Do you go to school early, like Sarah?
  Does Sarah like her life on the farm?

We make negatives with **do not** (**don't**) or **does not** (**doesn't**) + infinitive.
  Sarah and Jeff don't mind the hard work.
  Sarah doesn't often go to the city.

Use

For repeated actions, often with **always, often, sometimes, every day** etc.
  They often go to the river for a swim.

For facts which do not usually change.
  Sarah lives in Dalton, Australia.

Usually with verbs such as **like, love, hate; know, believe, understand; see, smell, hear; own, belong, have, need**.
  Sarah likes her life on the farm.
  Her parents own a sheep farm.

Adverbs of frequency

always, often, usually, sometimes, rarely and **never** come before the main verb but after **be**.
  They sometimes visit the platypus.
  It is usually hot.

every day/week, once a day/year usually come at the end or at the beginning.
  The sheep-shearing happens once a year.

Present continuous

Form

am/**are**/**is** + **ing** form
> he **is sorting**   they **are shearing**

The spelling sometimes changes before **ing**.
> take → tak**ing**   put → put**ting**

Questions and negatives:
> **Is** Sarah **working** in the wool-shed?
> Jeff **isn't helping** his father today.

Use

For something that is happening at the moment of speaking, often with **now**, **at the moment**, **just**, **today**.
> **At the moment**, Sarah's father **is working**.

For something that is happening for a limited time in the present, but not at the moment.
> He**'s reading** lots of books.

For future plans, often with time expressions such as **tomorrow**, **next year**, **next week**.
> Jeff **is going** to university **next year**.

1 Lifestyles

Make a list of five things that are the same in your life and in Sarah's life. Then make a list of five things that are different.

▷   *I live in the country, too.*
    I have a brother, too.

▷   *We don't own a farm.*
    We haven't got any sheep.

2 What is wrong?

The statements below are false. Correct them using negative sentences, like this:

▷   Sarah lives in a city.
    No, she doesn't, she lives in a small country town.
1   Sarah's father is a doctor.
2   Her parents own a goat farm.
3   Sarah has a sister.
4   At the moment Sarah is working with her mother.
5   Her brother is going to study French next year.
6   Over a thousand people live in Dalton.
7   Sarah is carrying the bad wool to the wool-store.
8   The school day finishes at three o'clock.

3 Sarah's life

a You are interviewing Sarah for an article in your school magazine.

Write ten questions you would like to ask her. Use the present simple. Read your questions to the class.

Ideas: her friends, her family, her school, her country, what she does in her spare time etc.

▷ *How old is your brother?*
▷ *Do you walk to school?*

b Write a short paragraph. Say what you like and what you don't like about Sarah's life.

▷ *I like Sarah's life on the farm because she looks after animals and she spends a lot of time outdoors. I wouldn't like to get up as early as she does . . .*

4 Australia: home of the kangaroo

Complete the sentences with a verb from the box in the correct form of the present simple or the present continuous. Use negative forms in some sentences.

be × 2	rain
help	own
enjoy	have
export	know
live	start
plan	read

▷ Sarah and her family *know* _____ most of the people in their town.

1 Most of Mr and Mrs Davis's friends _____ farmers.

2 Australia _____ fruit and wool.

3 Sarah's brother _____ lots of books at the moment.

4 Dalton _____ a very small population.

5 Sarah _____ at school at the moment.

   She _____ her father in the wool-shed.

6 Sarah and Jeff _____ swimming in the river.

7 In summer it is usually very hot, so school _____ early.

8 Kangaroos and koalas _____ in Australia.

9 The Davis family _____ the biggest sheep farm in Dalton.

   They _____ to buy more land next year.

10 It _____ in the summer in Dalton.

5 Follow that sheep

Work with a partner. Look at the pictures below.

Write a short story to describe what is happening in the pictures. Use the present simple and continuous, like this:

▷ *Sarah and Jeff are in the field. They are helping their father to get the sheep in. They are both wearing hats because it is very hot . . .*

6 Town or country?

Work in two teams. Have a class discussion. Team A supports country life. Team B supports city life. Team A makes a statement and Team B thinks of an argument against it.

First, make some notes. Here are some ideas to help you: family life, pollution, traffic, entertainment, shopping, crime.

▷ TEAM A *City traffic pollutes the air.*
Country life is healthier.

TEAM B *There isn't much traffic in the country, but that means there aren't many buses, so travelling is difficult.*

2 The sky went green

Past simple; Past continuous; Past simple and continuous

Everyone **thought** that Gulf Breeze in the USA **was** an ordinary, quiet little town until 11 November 1977. Two friends, Ed Walters and Charlie Bennett **reported** a very strange incident. At first nobody **believed** their story, but even today, both Charlie and Ed claim that the incident really **happened**. Here is part of an interview which was shown on Florida News the day after the kidnapping.

It **was** seven o'clock in the evening. My friend Charlie and I **were walking** through the park. We **were going** home. We **were talking** and **laughing**. Suddenly the sky **went** very dark. Charlie **looked** up and **said**, 'It's going to rain'. Then I **heard** a loud bang and the sky **went** bright green. I **thought** I **was dreaming**. There **was** a huge, shiny spaceship just above our heads. It **wasn't moving**. It **was pulling** us off the ground. Seconds later we **were** inside it. Twenty strange creatures **were looking** at us. They all **had** wrinkled skin and hands like pincers. They **didn't hurt** us. They **were smiling** and they **seemed** very friendly.

I don't know how long we **were** in space, but I think the spaceship **was moving**. Suddenly the door **opened** underneath us. We **fell** out of the spaceship onto the ground. We **were** back in the park again. Charlie and I just **stared** at each other. We **were shaking** because we **were** so scared. Then we **ran** home as fast as we **could**. That's all Charlie and I can remember. I know it sounds crazy but it's the truth.

On 11 November 1982, exactly five years after the kidnapping, more strange things **happened** in Gulf Breeze. Cars **disappeared**, cats **started** to fly and several people **saw** spaceships in the sky.

pincer

wrinkled

Grammar lesson

Past simple

Form

For regular verbs we add **ed** or **d**.
> open → open**ed**   believe → believe**d**

The spelling sometimes changes.
> stop → stop**ped**   try → tr**ied**

Irregular verbs have special forms. Look at the list at the back of the book.
> see → **saw**   go → **went**   take → **took**

We make questions with **did** + infinitive.
> *What **did** he **say**?*

We make negatives with **did not** (**didn't**) + infinitive.
> *They **didn't hurt** us.*

Use

For an action which started and finished in the past, often with a time expression (**suddenly**, **last week**, a date).
> *Suddenly the sky **went** very dark.*

Past continuous

Form

was/**were** + **ing** form
> *he **was walking**   we **were talking***

The spelling sometimes changes when we add **ing**.
> smile → smil**ing**   run → run**ning**

Questions and negatives:
> ***Were** the creatures **smiling**?*
> *The spaceship **wasn't moving**.*

Use

For an action that was happening, but not completed, at a particular time in the past. We often describe a scene with the past continuous.
> *Charlie **was talking** and Ed **was laughing**.*

We do not usually use these verbs in the past continuous:

be	have	know	like	see
seem	own	believe	love	smell
	belong	understand	hate	hear
		need		

Past simple and continuous

Sometimes one past action interrupts another. We use the past continuous for the action which was already happening and the past simple for the shorter 'interrupting' action.
> *I **was walking** through the park when suddenly I **heard** a loud bang.*

1   Quick quiz

Fit the past simple forms of these verbs into the puzzle. Write the answers across.

can	happen	see
talk	take	think

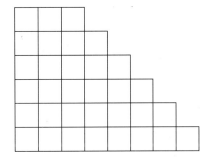

2   Scientific theory

After the incident, scientists tried to guess which planet the aliens were from.

Look at the statements below. If you think a statement is true, circle the letter in the true column, if you think it is false, circle the letter in the false column. Put together all the circled letters to find out which planet it could be.

	True	False
It happened late at night.	Z	T
Ed heard a loud bang.	R	E
Ed and Charlie live in Australia.	K	I
The aliens were unfriendly.	B	G
Ed can't remember everything.	L	E
The sky went dark green.	S	O
Charlie and Ed were scared.	N	D

The aliens came from planet _____

3 News flash

Work with a partner. Partner A is a television reporter. Partner B is Charlie. Use the table to ask and answer questions with the past simple and past continuous.

Partner A	Partner B
Where/you?	park
What/date?	11 November 1977
What/you/doing?	talk/laugh
Where/you/go?	home
How many/aliens?	twenty
What/aliens/look/like?	wrinkled/skin

▷ Where were you when this happened?
I was in the park.

4 Truth or fiction?

a Some other people in Gulf Breeze told reporters that they had seen the UFO. Look at the pictures and read what they told the reporter. Match the names of the speakers to the people.

BILL JACOBS   I was working in the garden when I saw a very bright light. I heard a loud noise. I went inside and locked the door.

JIM SHORT   I was driving my car when suddenly I heard a loud bang. I thought someone had crashed into my car.

PAM BAKER   I was at home watching TV. It was very late at night and I noticed that it was raining. Suddenly I heard a strange whistling noise. I looked out of the window and saw a huge object like an aeroplane flying through the sky.

BOB ROBBINS   I was walking with my dog in the fields when suddenly he started barking. It was getting dark but the sky was green. It was frightening, so we ran home.

b One of the people in (**a**) invented stories about the UFO. Read Ed's article again.

Who do you think was lying? Discuss the answer with a partner and write down the untrue statements.

1 _____
2 _____
3 _____
4 _____

c Read the questions very carefully, then say the answers.

1 What was Bill doing when he saw the light?
2 What did Pam do when she heard the noise?
3 What did Bob and his dog do when the sky went green?
4 What was Jim doing when he heard the bang?
5 What was Pam doing when she heard the noise?
6 What did Bill do when he saw the light?
7 What did Jim do when he heard the bang?
8 What were Bob and his dog doing when the sky went green?

5 Flying cats!

More mysterious things happened in Gulf Breeze ten years later. Mr Alan Rogers told the Gulf Breeze Daily News what had happened on the night of 11 November 1987.

Put the verbs in the past simple or past continuous.

I ▷ *was sitting* _____ (sit) at home,

having dinner with my wife when suddenly our cat, Toto, flew across the room.

My wife said, '1 _____ (do) you see that?' We 2 _____ (can) believe our eyes. Later, we

3 _____ (watch) TV and it

4 _____ (change) channel.

'5 _____ (do) you change the channel?' I asked my wife. 'No,' she said.

At ten o'clock we 6 _____ (wash up) when all the lights

7 _____ (go) out.

At first we 8 _____ (think) our

son David 9 _____ (try) to

frighten us. We 10 _____ (look)

in his bedroom but he was asleep.

We 11 _____ (stay) awake all night. It was very strange and very frightening.

6 Strange stories

Write a short paragraph about something strange that happened to you, or to someone you know. If you can't think of anything that really happened, invent a story.

Use the past simple and the past continuous.

▷ *One Friday afternoon, I was talking to my friend when suddenly . . .*

7 Play the game

Work with a partner. Write the first part of a sentence using the past continuous + **when** on a piece of paper, like this:

▷ *I was walking down the street when . . .*

Fold the paper so that the first part of the sentence is at the back, like this:

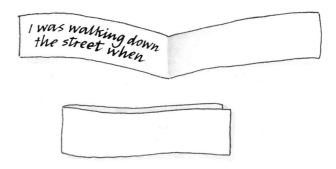

Exchange papers with your partner. Don't read what's on the paper!

Write the second part of the sentence using **suddenly** + past simple, like this:

▷ *. . . suddenly I saw a dragon driving a car.*

Now read out the two parts of the sentence to the class.

▷ *I was playing tennis when suddenly the sky went purple.*
▷ *I was doing my homework when suddenly I saw a green monster.*

3 Mystery monsters
Present perfect simple; Present perfect continuous; **for** and **since**

Wanted

Have you **seen** the Loch Ness Monster? Thousands of people **have reported** seeing a large animal in the famous lake called Loch Ness in Scotland. **For** fourteen centuries people **have been trying** to capture it, but perhaps it **has been living** in the lake even longer. Although local people **have** always **talked** about the mysterious creature, it is only in the last sixty years that there **has been** any evidence that it might exist. In 1933, John McGregor, a local businessman, saw the lake bubbling and a huge object with two humps came out of the water.

Since that day, scientists **have been searching** the lake with underwater equipment, trying to find out what kind of animal lives there. Unfortunately, they **haven't managed** to find it **yet** because the lake is so deep and so dark.

Tourists from all over the world **have visited** Loch Ness, hoping to see the monster. They **have** even **given** it a nickname: 'Nessie'. Many people **have taken** photographs of it, although experts **have proved** that some of the photos are forgeries. Scientists **have suggested** that the Loch Ness monster is a dinosaur which was trapped in the lake during the Ice Age. Your help is needed to solve the mystery. Please contact the *Loch Ness Research Centre, Inverness, Scotland* if you **have ever seen** it.

Here is a description of the monster:

The Loch Ness Monster

Length	About 50 metres including tail.
Body	About 30 metres long, with at least two humps.
Head	Half horse, half snake and quite small.
Neck	Long and thin, like a giraffe.
Tail	Very long and pointed at the end.
Colour	Yellowish-brown.
Food	People have said that it hunts sheep on land but it also eats underwater plants.
Character	Shy, doesn't like to be seen very often.
Habitat	Lives in the deepest and coldest part of the lake, approximately 1 km from the surface.

Grammar lesson

Present perfect simple

Form

have or **has** + past participle
> there **has been**
> **have** you **seen**?
> they **haven't managed**

Look at the back of the book for a list of irregular verbs and their past participles.

Use

For a completed action with **just** and **already**, and in sentences with **not . . . yet**.
> They **haven't managed** to find it **yet**.

For a completed action which has an effect or result in the present.
> People **have given** it a nickname.
> (Result: Some people call it 'Nessie'.)

For a completed action at an unknown or unstated time, often with **ever** and **never**.
> Please contact the Centre if you **have ever seen** it.

With verbs that are not usually used in the continuous, such as **be**, **have**, **know**, **like**, **see**.
> **Have** you **seen** the Loch Ness Monster?

Present perfect continuous

Form

have been or **has been** + **ing** form
> it **has been living**
> **have** they **been trying**?
> they **haven't been searching**

Use

For an action that began in the past and continues up to the present. It may be finished or unfinished.
> Scientists **have been searching** the lake.

Often with verbs that show long actions, such as **play**, **learn**, **read**, **do**, **wait**, **live**, **rain**, **work**, **sleep**.
> Perhaps it **has been living** in the lake even longer.

for and since

We use **for** and **since**, usually with a verb in the present perfect continuous, to say how long something has been happening.

We use **for** for a length of time and **since** for a point of time in the past.
> People have been looking for the monster
> **for** fourteen centuries/**since** the fifth century.

1 Interview at the Research Centre

a Imagine you are a scientist at the Loch Ness Research Centre. You are going to interview someone who says that they have been watching the monster for several years. Write ten questions you would like to ask this person, like this:

> ▷ *How many times have you seen the monster?*
> ▷ *Have you taken any photographs of it?*

b Work with a partner. Take turns to ask and answer the questions you have written.

2 Beware of the Kraken

Match the two halves of each sentence to find out about another monster.

▷   It is a
1   I have spent ten years of
2   People have been frightened of the
3   Hundreds of sailors have written about the Kraken
4   They have told stories about their friends
5   People say that the Kraken has lived in the North
6   Scientists have calculated
7   For the past three months I have been
8   I haven't found it

travelling round the world looking for the Kraken.
Sea as well as in the Atlantic Ocean.
that the Kraken is 30 metres wide.
my life trying to find a monster called the Kraken.
sea monster.
Kraken since the 17th century.
yet, but I will!
being attacked and eaten by the Kraken.
destroying their ships.

3 Footprints in the snow

Complete with the correct form of the present perfect simple or the present perfect continuous.

'I'm reading a book about monsters,' Ben told Nick one day.
'I ▷ *have been reading* (read) it for a week now. It's all about people who 1_____ (see) strange things. There are reports about the research which experts 2_____ (do). The Yeti is a famous monster. People 3_____ (look for) a 'wild man' in the Himalayas for years. Several people 4_____ (find) enormous footprints in the snow – half a metre long, with three small toes and one huge toe. Travellers 5_____ (explore) Tibet for years, and there 6_____ (be) several sightings of large animals. In the book it says that a woman called Dr Sharp 7_____ (travel) to Mongolia several times and 8_____ (collect) proof that yetis also live there. She believes that a yeti is a Neanderthal man.'

'You mean, she thinks that Neanderthal man 9_____ (survive)?' Nick asked. 'When you 10_____ (finish) the book, can I borrow it?'

4 The wanted poster

a Work with a partner. Design your own wanted poster. Draw a picture to show what your monster looks like.

b Write a short paragraph. Use the present perfect simple and continuous to describe where your monster lives, how many times it has been seen, what it looks like and why you need to find it, like this:

> *Our monster lives in the desert. It has only been seen ten times. It has attacked other animals. People have said that it eats human beings . . .*

c Read your paragraph to the class and show them the picture. The class votes for the most imaginative wanted poster.

5 Monster game

Work in two teams. Invent as many correct sentences as you can. For each sentence you must use one phrase from each box. Your sentences can be funny or serious.

Use the present perfect simple or the present perfect continuous of the verbs in Box 2. Remember that **already**, **never** and **often** go *after* **have**, **do** and **be** but *before* the main verb.

Take turns to read out your sentences. Your team gets one point for each correct sentence.

> *A dinosaur has been living in New York for centuries.*

Box 1	Box 2
Nessie	eat
the Minotaur	see
the Yeti	live
an alien	swim
the Kraken	hunt
a dragon	sleep
a television reporter	work
a dinosaur	take

Box 3	Box 4
tourist(s)	since 1925
photograph(s)	many times
underground	never
peanut(s)	for three weeks
monster(s)	already
at the supermarket	since yesterday
in New York	for centuries
television(s)	often

What is it like to have money, fame, a career and fans when you are only ten?

Have you ever **dreamt** of becoming a Hollywood child star, like Macaulay Culkin perhaps? Since the age of ten, he **has been** world famous as Kevin in the 'Home Alone' comedies. He **earned** over a million dollars for each film.

Scott Perry is ten and he has dreams of becoming famous, too. He **hasn't had** a big film role yet, but he **has appeared** in TV commercials. Scott told 'Blockbusters' magazine about his first commercial:

'Two years ago I **got** a part in a commercial for ice-cream. I **had to** eat four big spoonfuls of strawberry ice-cream in twenty seconds. At first it **tasted** fine, but when my TV 'mother' **brought** in the ice-cream for the sixteenth time, I **started** to feel sick and **had to** run out of the studio! I **haven't eaten** ice-cream since then.'

commercial short advertising film

Grammar lesson

Present perfect simple

Form [See Chapter 3]

Use

For a finished action at an unknown or unstated time, often with **ever**, **never**, **just** and **not yet**.

> Scott **has appeared** in TV commercials.
> **Have** you ever **dreamt** of becoming a star?
> He **hasn't had** a big film role yet.

Past simple

Form [See Chapter 2]

Use

For an action that started and finished in the past, often with a time expression (**ago**, **last year**, **in 1990**, **at first** etc.).

> Two years ago I **got** a part in a TV commercial for ice-cream.
> At first it **tasted** fine.

We use the past simple, not the present perfect simple, to talk about things that happened in the past.

1 Word search

Look for past simple forms and past participles. How many of each can you find? Write two lists.

F	S	A	W	K	D	B	J
E	A	T	E	N	O	E	T
S	P	O	K	E	N	E	A
A	I	O	X	W	E	N	T
T	Y	K	N	O	W	N	E

2 An interview with Scott

A year later Scott starred in an adventure film called 'Journey to Nowhere'.

Harry Sinclair, a TV journalist, is talking to Scott about his career. Complete the sentences with the present perfect simple or the past simple of the verb in brackets.

HARRY Scott, how ▷ _did you get_

(you get) the role of Tim in 'Journey to Nowhere'?

SCOTT I ¹_____ (be) lucky. The

film director ²_____ (need)

an eleven-year-old boy with blond hair,

freckles and big teeth. I had all those

things!

HARRY How long ³_____ (it take)

to make the film?

SCOTT It ⁴_____ (take) only eight

weeks. We ⁵_____ (film)

most of it in the summer holidays two

years ago.

HARRY Is it true that you ⁶_____

(have) role offers from ten other big film

companies?

SCOTT Yes. Last week I ⁷_____

(get) an offer to play a computer genius

who makes everything go wrong with

business computers all over the world.

It's very funny.

HARRY Scott, you ⁸_____ (earn) a

lot of money, and you're only thirteen.

What ⁹_____ (you do)

with it?

SCOTT Well, I ¹⁰_____ (buy) a

yacht, a zoo, and a new house for my

parents.

3 A film I have seen

a Say your answers round the class.

1 What is the name of the best film you have ever seen?
2 How long ago did you see it?
3 Who were the stars?
4 What kind of roles did they play?
5 What kind of film was it?
  a science fiction film?
  a fantasy film?
  an adventure film?
  a family comedy?

b Work with a partner. Interview each other about your favourite film. Ask and answer ten questions.

▷ *When did you see the film?*
  I saw it a year ago.
▷ *What did you like most?*
  I liked the main actor and the special effects.

c With your partner, write a short paragraph about a film you both enjoyed. When you have finished, read your paragraph to the class.

4 My name is Jesse Jones

Imagine you are child star Jesse Jones. Round the class, take it in turns to say what you have done in your life so far.

They can be serious or funny things. Play the game like this:

▷ PUPIL A *My name is Jesse Jones. I have made six films.*
▷ PUPIL B *My name is Jesse Jones. I have made six films and I have bought an old castle.*
▷ PUPIL C *. . . have made six films, I have bought an old castle and I have met the President of the USA.*

Continue.

5 Junior genius   Past perfect simple; Past perfect continuous

James Stoker was fifteen years old when he became the youngest fully qualified doctor in the United States. James was a genius. By the age of two he **had learnt** to read and write. Before his sixth birthday his father **had taught** him to speak three languages fluently and he could play the violin and the piano perfectly. James spent all his time reading and studying. After he **had passed** his school-leaving exams at the age of nine, he went to college. A year and a half later, he **had finished** college and started at a medical school. At the age of twelve, he didn't know what football was, because nobody **had taught** him how to play. There **hadn't been** time.

At fifteen, he was ready to take the final examination. On the morning of the exam, although he **had been studying** for 48 hours, he wasn't tired. After the exam he walked through the park, but he didn't arrive home until seven o'clock in the evening, very tired and very dirty. What **had** he **been doing**? his mother wondered. He **had met** some eight-year-olds in the park. They **had been teaching** him how to play football.

> **genius** a person who has a great ability, usually at an early age
>
> **expert** a person who knows a lot about a subject, or who knows how to do something very well

Grammar lesson

Past perfect simple

Form

had + past participle for all persons
> He **had learnt** to read.
> **Had** he **passed** his exams?
> There **hadn't been** time.

Use

For a past action which happened before another past action, often with **after**, **when**, **because** or **as soon as**.
> After he **had passed** his school-leaving exams at the age of nine, he went to college.
> He didn't know what football was, because nobody **had taught** him how to play.

Past perfect continuous

Form

had been + **ing** form for all persons
> They **had been teaching** him.
> What **had** he **been doing**?
> He **hadn't been studying**.

Use

For a past action which continued until another past action happened, often with verbs that describe actions which can take a long time, such as **play**, **learn**, **read**, **do**, **wait**, **live**, **rain**, **work**, **sleep**.
> What **had** he **been doing**?
> He **had been playing** football.

1 Facts about James

Choose **a**, **b** or **c** to complete the sentences about James. Say your answers.

▷ James's teachers were amazed. They ___*a*___ a pupil like him before.

   a had never met
   b never met
   c have never met

1 He ____ to read and write by the time he was two.
   a learnt
   b had learnt
   c had been learning

2 When James started school at five, he ____ to playschool.

   a didn't go
   b hadn't been
   c had been going

3 He ____ school by the age of nine.

   a was leaving
   b had left
   c had been leaving

4 As soon as he ____ college, he went to medical school.

   a had finished
   b was finishing
   c finished

5 Before he started medical school, he ____ twenty books on anatomy.

   a had already read
   b already read
   c had already been reading

6 He ____ a ball in his life before he played football with the eight-year-olds.

   a had never kicked
   b never kicked
   c had been kicking

> **amazed** extremely surprised
>
> **anatomy** the study of the human body

2 Because . . .

Write ten sentences about James with **because** and a verb in the past perfect simple, like this:

▷ *James couldn't play football because he hadn't learnt to play as a child.*

3 What had he been doing?

When he was sixteen, James decided to try some of the things he had never done before. Look at the picture clues. Write down what James had been doing.

▷ *He had been smoking.*

4 Another genius

Work with a partner. Invent a story about another amazing child genius. Write the story of his/her life in a short paragraph. Use the past perfect and words and phrases such as **by the time**, **at the age of**, **after**, **before**, **as soon as**.

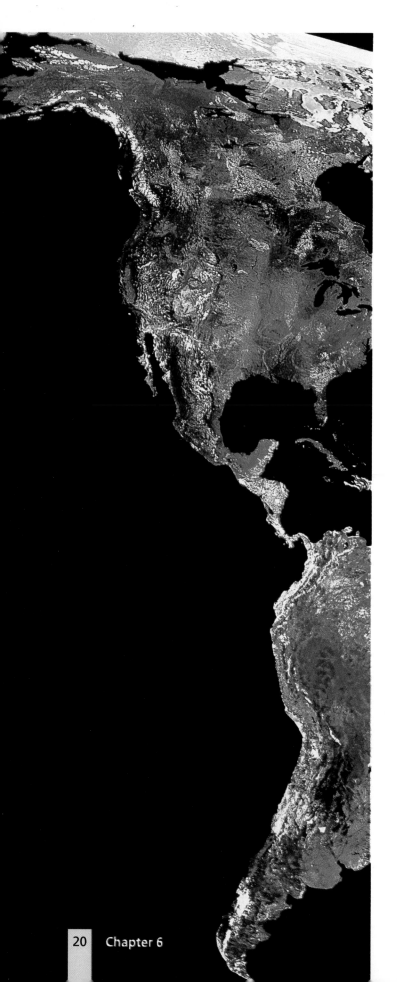

Pam and Ted Gibbs **are about to go** on an unusual holiday. They **are going to travel** from Alaska to Tierra del Fuego, a distance of 25,665 kilometres – on motorbikes.

PAM We **fly** to Anchorage at ten o'clock tomorrow morning and this time next week we**'ll be travelling** down the Canadian coast. We**'re taking** the shortest route along the west coast.

TED I expect we**'ll have** problems with bad weather and bad roads. We**'ll break down**, of course, so we**'re taking** spare parts with us.

PAM The weather forecast for Alaska is fine at the moment, so we**'re going to have** a good start.

TED We **will be travelling** up to 250 kilometres a day on good roads, but on bad roads we **won't be able to** get very far. We know that it **won't be** an easy trip. We'd like to spend Christmas at home, but we **won't have arrived** back in England by then.

PAM When we get back, we **will have been travelling** for over a year. That's a long time, but we **will have made** a dream come true.

TED That's right. But we**'ll** probably never **want** to ride a motorbike again!

spare parts extra parts for a machine

tough hard, difficult

Grammar lesson

The future

There are many ways of talking about future time. It depends what we want to express. We use the following forms.

Present simple

For timetables and travel arrangements.

> We *fly* to Anchorage at ten o'clock tomorrow morning.

Present continuous or **be going to**

For an intention or a plan.

> We're *taking* spare parts with us.
> They **are going to travel** from Alaska to Tierra del Fuego.

be going to

For a prediction when something in the present tells us about the future.

> The weather in Alaska is fine now, so we're *going to have* a good start.

will ('ll) and won't

For a prediction.

> On bad roads we **won't be able to** get very far.

After **expect**, **hope**, **think**, **be afraid** and with **probably**.

> I **expect** we'll have problems with bad weather.
> We'll **probably** never **want** to ride a motorbike again!

be about to

For an action in the very near future.

> Pam and Ted **are about to go** on an unusual holiday.

Future continuous

Form **will be** + **ing** form

For a routine or repeated action over a length of time in the future.

> We **will be travelling** up to 250 kilometres a day.

For an action which will be happening at a particular point of time in the future.

> This time next week we'll **be travelling** down the Canadian coast.

Future perfect simple

Form **will have** + past participle

For an action that will be completed at a particular time in the future, often with **by** + point of time (**by then**, **by next year**, **by 1999**).

> We **won't have arrived by then**.

Future perfect continuous

Form **will have been** + **ing** form

For an action that starts in the future and continues up to a particular time in the future, often with **for** + length of time.

> When we get back, we **will have been travelling for** over a year.

1 Right or wrong?

Say whether the statements are right or wrong. Correct the wrong statements.

▷ Ted and Pam are about to leave for Alaska.
Right.
▷ They are going to travel from Alaska to New York.
Wrong. They are going to travel from Alaska to Tierra del Fuego.

1 They are flying to Vancouver.
2 Their flight leaves at eight o'clock tomorrow.
3 They will be travelling by bicycle.
4 The weather in Alaska is going to be bad.
5 They are taking spare parts for the motorbikes.
6 They will be travelling over 200 kilometres a day.
7 They will be away for over a year.
8 They will have arrived home by Christmas.
9 By the end of their trip, they will have driven 10,000 kilometres.
10 They are planning to go on another trip.

2 Travel game

a Work with a partner.

Partner A chooses an adventure trip. Partner B must guess which trip it is by asking questions with **be going to**.

Imagine Partner A is going to . . .

cross Thailand by bicycle
cross Alaska by sledge
ride across the Alps on a donkey
walk across Mexico
hitch-hike through India

▷ PARTNER B *Are you going to learn Spanish?*
    PARTNER A *No, I'm not.*
    PARTNER B *Is it going to be very cold on your trip?*

Reverse roles and play the game again.

b Suggest five more adventure trips and write them on the board.

A pupil chooses a trip and the class guesses it by asking questions with **be going to**.

3 What will they need?

a Every night Pam and Ted will camp in their tent. Which things will they need? Which things won't they need? Say your answers.

a medical kit	a Chinese dictionary
a tennis racket	a trumpet
a tin-opener	a compass
a computer	maps
matches	skis
a suitcase	soap

▷ *They will need a medical kit.*
▷ *They won't need a tennis racket.*

b Some very important things are missing. What else will they need? Think of five more things.

▷ *They'll need sleeping bags.*

c Imagine that Pam and Ted are going to fly from Anchorage to Tierra del Fuego instead of taking their motorbikes. What five things wouldn't they need to take with them?

4 Amazing records

Complete the news stories with **will/won't** or with a form of **be going to**.

Pete Newman, a 20-year-old Canadian, ▷ *is going to* walk across Canada. He thinks he ▷ *will* be able to complete his walk from Vancouver to Halifax in 95 days.

Five French sailors ___1___ sail round the world on a catamaran. They hope that they ___2___ complete their trip in only 79 days. If they succeed, they ___3___ set a new world record. Jean Dubois told our reporter, 'It ___4___ be an easy journey. Our worst problem ___5___ probably be seasickness.'

Sheila Wood, an 18-year-old student from Penzance, ___6___ travel over 11,000 kilometres around the British coast – in roller boots. She ___7___ be the first person to do this. Sheila, who ___8___ nineteen next Monday, told our reporter, 'The trip ___9___ take me about six months. My biggest problem ___10___ be loneliness. I'm sure that this adventure ___11___ teach me a lot about myself.' Before she starts, Sheila ___12___ buy several pairs of spare wheels for her boots.

---

5 Back home

a Ted and Pam are going to take the shortest route from Alaska to Tierra del Fuego. When they return, which countries will/won't they have travelled through? If you are not sure, look in an atlas. Say your answers.

Mexico Egypt Japan Canada Greece
Brazil Peru Turkey Panama Ecuador

  ▷ *They will have travelled through Mexico.*
  ▷ *They won't have travelled through Egypt.*

b Can you name three more countries which they will have travelled through?

6 The trip of a lifetime

a Work with a partner. You are going to cross your country on foot, by bicycle, on camels etc. Plan your route, then write a paragraph about your plans. What will you be doing and when? What will you be taking with you?

  ▷ *We will be leaving from . . . by bicycle on 1 July. We won't be taking very much luggage with us. My friend will be carrying the food and I . . .*

b Read your paragraph to the class.

Who will be having the most interesting or most exciting trip? Take a vote.

NICK   I'm going to the cinema tonight – with a friend.

JENNY   Oh? **Who** have you invited? Or rather, **who** has invited you?

NICK   Jane has invited me. **Do** you want to come too?

JENNY   **What film** are you going to see? And **which cinema** is it on at? The Regent or the Odeon?

NICK   The Odeon. The film's called 'Mystery Man'.

JENNY   I think I'd rather stay here and watch TV.

NICK   Again? You're an addict. **Haven't** you got anything better to do?

JENNY   **Why shouldn't** I watch TV if I want to? **What** are you looking **for**?

NICK   The TV guide. **Have** you seen it?

JENNY   No, I haven't. Anyway, **who watches** TV most in our house? You do! And **what happens** if you miss your sports programme? You get bad-tempered. You're the TV addict, not me! **Why don't** you go out and leave me alone?

NICK   I don't want to go out any more. I want to watch 'Football Special'. **Which channel** is it **on**? I've got an idea. **Why don't** we all watch TV?

addict a person who cannot do without something
bad-tempered in a bad mood, angry

Grammar lesson

Questions

In yes/no questions the auxiliary verb comes first, then the subject and main verb.

Do	you want to come too?	Yes/No.
Have	you seen the TV guide?	Yes/No.

Questions which ask for information begin with question words: **where**, **when**, **what**, **who**, **which**, **why**, **whose**, **how**, **how much/many**, **how often**, **what time**, **what kind of** etc. We put the question word before the auxiliary verb.

Where	's	the TV guide?
Who	has	invited you?

If **who** or **what** is the subject, the verb in the question is the same as in an affirmative sentence.
> *Who watches TV most?*
> *What happens if you miss your programme?*

If **who** or **what** is the object, the verb is the same as in a yes/no question.
> *What do you want?*

Compare:
> *Who has invited you?* (**Who** is the subject.)
> *Who have you invited?* (**Who** is the object.)

If there is a preposition in the question, it usually goes at the end.
> *What are you looking for?*
> *Which channel is it on?*

what or which?

We use **what** and **which** with or without a noun.
> *What film are you going to see?*
> *Which do you like best?*

We usually use **what** if there are many possible answers and **which** if there are only a few.
> *What are you going to do tonight?*
> *Which cinema is it on at? The Regent or the Odeon?*

We usually use **which** with people, even if there are a lot of possible answers.
> *Which TV stars do you like best?*

Negative questions

To make a negative question we add **n't** to the auxiliary verb.

Negative questions can express surprise, regret or annoyance.
> *Haven't you got anything better to do?*
> *Why shouldn't I watch TV if I want to?*

Suggestions

With **Why don't we/you . . . ?** we can make suggestions.
> *Why don't we all watch TV?*

1 Quick quiz

Can you do this puzzle in two minutes? Put in the missing question words.

1. is going to the cinema?
2. cinema are you going to?
3. don't we watch television?
4. 's the TV guide?
5. 's on Channel 4?
6. does the film start?
7. many films are on TV today?
8. favourite programme is 'Football Special'?

2 Your favourite TV programme

A pupil thinks of a popular TV series or programme. The class asks questions and tries to guess it. The pupil gives only one clue to each question. Read these questions and use them to guess the programme.

What is it about?
Who is it about?
What does the main actor/actress look like?
Which channel is it on?
Which day is it on?

▷ CLASS *What is it about?*
PUPIL *A detective/a family/animals.*
CLASS *Which day is it on?*
PUPIL *Tuesday/every day.*

3 Are you a TV addict?

a Complete the questionnaire with the correct form of the missing auxiliary verb, **do**, **be**, **have** or **can**, **would** etc.

b Work with a partner. Ask each other the questions and tick (✓) the Yes or No box. Then count the Yes answers. If you have . . .

TV questionnaire

	Yes	No
▷ _Do_ you watch TV for more than two hours a day?	✓	
Have you got a TV set in your room?		✓
1 _____ television part of your daily routine?		
2 _____ you sometimes watch TV because you have nothing else to do?		
3 _____ you always turn on the TV if you are alone?		
4 _____ you be miserable without a TV set?		
5 _____ you ever stayed at home to watch TV instead of going out with friends?		
6 _____ you sometimes dream about someone on a TV programme?		
7 _____ you name four TV detective series?		
8 _____ you disappointed if there's nothing on TV that really interests you?		
9 _____ it difficult for you to turn the TV off?		
10 _____ television take up more than half your free time?		

Results

1 to 3:
You have a healthy attitude towards television.

4 to 6:
Be careful! Remember, there's more to life than television.

7 to 10:
You could be a TV addict. Try to do more outdoor activities and only watch two programmes a day.

4 What do you watch?

Put in **who**, **what** or **which**.

▷ _What_ did you watch on TV last night?

1 _____ watches TV most in your family?

2 _____ happens if the TV breaks down in the middle of an exciting programme?

3 _____ kind of programmes do you like best?

4 _____'s your favourite TV personality?

5 _____ channel is your favourite programme on?

6 _____ time does your favourite programme start?

7 _____ TV actors do you like best?

8 _____ TV channels do you watch most?

9 _____ do you do when there are two good programmes on TV at the same time?

10 _____ likes to watch the same TV programmes as you?

5 Family matters

a Write as many questions as you can about the picture. Check them with your teacher.

> ▷ *What is the family doing?*
> ▷ *How many people are there in the family?*
> ▷ *Does the mother look angry?*

b Make two teams. Close your books. Take turns to ask and answer questions about the picture.

6 A good solution?

Read how Mary Williams solved her family's viewing problems.

Two years ago, Mary Williams from Cardiff did what many other mothers threaten to do, but never do. She threw away the family's television set!

The Williamses have three children. Mary knew that they would all be very cross about missing their favourite programmes, and she was right. At first they spent all their free time watching television at their friends' houses, but after a while they began listening to more music, reading and playing sports after school. Mary knew that the children would soon get used to living without the television.

> **threaten** express an intention to do something unpleasant to someone

a Write five questions about the text.

> ▷ *What did Mary Williams do two years ago?*

b Discuss these questions in class:

1 Do you think it was right of Mary to throw away the TV set?
2 How would you feel if it happened in your family?
3 Are there other solutions?

8 Sweet dreams Question tags; Short answers

NICK I had one of my amazing dreams again last night, Jenny.

JENNY You haven't had a dream like that for a very long time, **have you?**

NICK **No, I haven't.**

JENNY It means you are very imaginative, **doesn't it?**

NICK I'm not sure, but this dream was even more amazing than the others. I dreamt that I was a cowboy in Colorado. I had to move 200 cattle to an area eighty miles away without any help. The dream was so realistic that I could feel the heat of the sun and hear the cows. It took three days and each evening I made a camp near a river and slept by the fire with my rifle.

JENNY You do have some amazing dreams, **don't you?** Did you get there safely with the cattle in the end?

NICK **Yes, I did.** I arrived at seven o'clock and stayed there that night. It really was a great adventure. I didn't want to wake up! Dreams don't last long enough, **do they?**

JENNY **No, they don't.** Not when they are as exciting as yours!

cattle another word for cows

Grammar lesson

Question tags

We often use a question tag to ask for agreement with a statement.

Sometimes it is not a real question, because we already know the answer, and the voice goes down.
> *You do have some amazing dreams, **don't you?***

If it is a real question, because we are not sure, the voice goes up.
> *It means you are very imaginative, **doesn't it?***

A question tag always ends with **I**, **you**, **he**, **she**, **it** etc. or **there**.

If the statement is affirmative, the question tag is negative. If the statement is negative, the question tag is affirmative.

If the statement verb is **be**, **have**, **do**, **can**, **must**, **should** etc., we repeat it in the question tag.
> *You haven't had a dream like that for a very long time, **have you?***

With other verbs (**eat**, **go**, **talk**, **work** etc.) we use a form of **do** in the present simple and past simple.
> *You had a really exciting dream last night, **didn't you?***

Short answers

It is not polite to answer a question with **Yes** or **No** alone. It is usual to add a short answer. We use the verb from the question.
> *Did you get there safely?*
> **Yes, I did./No, I didn't.**
> *Was the dream very realistic?*
> **Yes, it was./No, it wasn't.**

1 Some facts about dreams

Complete the sentences with the correct question tag.

▷ Some people think they can see the future through their dreams, *don't they?*

1 Dreams show that you are very imaginative, _____

2 We dream during light sleep, _____

3 If you wake up while you are dreaming, you can often remember the dream, _____

4 A frightening dream is called a nightmare, _____

5 Men don't dream as much as women, _____

6 Eating cheese late at night makes you dream, _____

7 Sometimes your true thoughts come out in your dreams, _____

8 Sigmund Freud wrote books about dreams, _____

9 Some people talk while they are dreaming, _____

10 Most dreams don't come true, _____

2 Remembering your dreams

a In a short paragraph, write down the details of a dream that you once had. If you can't remember a dream, invent one.

b Read your dream to the class. When you have finished, test the class to see if they can remember all the details. The class uses a question tag, you use short answers.

▷ CLASS *In your dream you were eating a giant ice-cream, weren't you?*
YOU *Yes, I was.*
CLASS *Suddenly it began to melt, didn't it?*
YOU *Yes, it did.*

3 Dream pictures

Look at the pictures on the right for two minutes. Try to remember as much as possible about them. Close your books. A pupil chooses a picture. The class tries to guess which picture it is by asking yes/no questions. The pupil keeps his or her book open and gives short answers.

▷ CLASS *Is there a tree in the picture?*
PUPIL *Yes, there is.*

NICK   Jenny, shall we go into the reptile house?

JENNY   Oh, all right, but I hate snakes and lizards. I've got a phobia about them.

NICK   **So has** Ben. I asked him if he would like to come in with us, but he refused.

JENNY   I don't like it here. It would be awful if a snake escaped. Is that possible?

NICK   I **don't suppose so**. They're all behind glass. Look at this lizard. You can hardly see it when it's on that branch. Do you think that's to protect it from its enemies?

JENNY   I **expect so**. Did you notice that it was a different colour when it was lying on those leaves in the corner?

NICK   Yes, I did. Look at this snake! It's at least five metres long. I'm glad it's behind glass: I wouldn't like to meet one in the wild.

JENNY   **Neither would** I! I thought you weren't scared, Nick.

NICK   Don't be silly! Of course I'm not scared. Look at those crocodiles.

JENNY   They're huge! I wonder how much they eat every day. Nick, you look awful. Would you like to leave?

NICK   Yes, I **think so**. We shouldn't have come in here. I'm going to have bad dreams about being chased by hungry crocodiles!

phobia   a strong dislike or fear of something

Grammar lesson

so/neither do I etc.

We use **so** to agree with affirmative statements and **neither** to agree with negative statements.

If **be**, **have**, **do**, **can**, **could**, **should**, **will** or **must** etc. is used in the original statement, we use a form of the same verb after **so** or **neither**.

'I've got a phobia about snakes.' 'So has Ben.'
'I wouldn't like to meet one in the wild.'
'Neither would I.'

But if the verb in the statement is an ordinary verb (**hate**, **like**, **enjoy**, **know** etc.) or **used to**, we use a form of **do** after **so** and **neither**.

Jenny didn't like the reptile house.
Neither did Nick.

I think so etc.

We also make short answers with **so** with the verbs **think**, **believe**, **expect**, **hope**, **suppose** and **be afraid**. We cannot leave out **so**.

'Do you think that's to protect it?' 'I expect so.'

The following negative forms are usual.

I **don't think so**.	I **hope not**.
I **don't expect so**.	I'm **afraid not**.
I **don't suppose so**.	

'Is that possible?' 'I don't suppose so.'

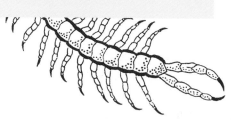

1 Spiders, snakes . . .

Match the correct short answers to the sentences, then say the sentences and the answers.

▷   I haven't got a phobia.   So do I.
1   I'm scared of spiders.   Neither would I.
2   I wouldn't touch a snake.   So have I.
3   I can't stand heights.   Neither will I.
4   I'm not frightened of mice.   So would I.
5   I can pick up a tarantula.   Neither can I.
6   I have a phobia about heights.   So am I.
7   I'll never have a pet bat.   Neither am I.
8   I would be scared if I saw a wasp. Neither do I.
9   I run as fast as I can if I see a rat. So can I.
10 I don't like long, dark tunnels.   Neither have I.

---

2 Likes and dislikes

Complete the short answers with the correct verb.

▷   Jenny doesn't like spiders.
    Neither _does_ Ann.

1   Jane can't stand worms.
    Neither _____ Jenny.

2   Ann hates snakes.
    So _____ Jenny.

3   Ben used to collect worms.
    So _____ Nick.

4   Sarah isn't scared of insects.
    Neither _____ Tom and Richard.

5   Ben can't stand spiders.
    Neither _____ Nick.

6   Jenny likes mice.
    So _____ Jane and Amanda.

7   Ann has a phobia.
    So _____ many people.

8   Jenny won't watch snakes on TV.
    Neither _____ Sarah and Richard.

9   Amanda is afraid of bats.
    So _____ her mother.

10 Nick doesn't like rats.
    Neither _____ Ben.

3 What frightens you?

Work with a partner. Most people are afraid of something. With your partner, find two things on the list that you are or used to be afraid of, and two things that you aren't or have never been afraid of.

deep water   dogs   fire
horses   lightning   thunder
spiders   snakes   flying
wasps   being alone darkness
heights   climbing ladders
crowded lifts

Take turns to tell the class, like this:

▷   *I'm not afraid of lightning, and neither is X.*
▷   *I used to be afraid of horses, and so did X.*

4 Horrible things?

Look at the pictures in this chapter. Work in small groups. One pupil writes the names of the other pupils in the group across the paper, and the 'horrible' things in the chapter down the paper, like this:

	Name X	Name Y	Name Z
bats	√		√
rats	×	×	×

Pass the paper round the group. If you like the thing, put a √. If you don't like the thing, put a ×. Take turns to tell the results to the class.

▷   *X likes bats. So does Z.*
▷   *X doesn't like rats. Neither do Y and Z.*

JENNY   Can you solve this puzzle about six brothers?

Ken is **older than** Bill and Ted. Ted is older than Sam. George is **younger than** Bill but older than Sam. George is younger than Ted. Ken is younger than John –

NICK   Stop, not so fast. Is Ted **as old as** Ken? And who's the **youngest**?

JENNY   I don't know. That's what you have to work out.

NICK   Can't you find a puzzle that's **easier** and **quicker** to do? I'm busy.

JENNY   It's one of the **easiest**. The others are all **more difficult**.

NICK   I've got a **bigger** and **better** book **than** that. The puzzles are much **more interesting**. I'll fetch it. We can solve the one about the brothers later.

Grammar lesson

Comparison of adjectives

We compare two people or things with the comparative form + **than**:
   *Ken is **younger than** John.*
or with (**not**) **as** . . . **as**:
   *Ken isn't **as old as** John.*

We compare three or more people or things with the superlative form.
   *Bill is young, Ted is younger. Is George the **youngest**?*

Adjective	Comparative	Superlative
One-syllable adjectives		
young	young**er**	young**est**
nice	nic**er**	nic**est**
With one vowel and one consonant:		
big	bi**gger**	bi**ggest**
Two-syllable adjectives		
boring	**more** boring	**most** boring
modern	**more** modern	**most** modern
But if the ending is **y**:		
easy	eas**ier**	eas**iest**

We also use **er** and **est** with **clever**, **gentle**, **narrow**, **quiet** and **simple**.

Adjectives with three or more syllables		
difficult	**more** difficult	**most** difficult
Irregular comparisons		
good	**better**	**best**
bad	**worse**	**worst**
far	**further**	**furthest**

1 What's the solution?

a Can you solve Jenny's puzzle about the six brothers? Here's an extra clue: Ted isn't as old as Bill. Write the names of the brothers on a piece of paper, from the youngest to the oldest.

b Check your solution with the class, then use it to complete the statements. Write a form of **old** or **young** and **than** or **as . . . as**.

▷ John is *the oldest* .

1 George is _____ Ted.

2 Ted isn't _____ Ken.

3 Ken isn't _____ George.

4 Bill isn't _____ Ken.

5 Sam is _____ .

2 What do they look like?

Look at the picture on page 32. What are the differences between the brothers ? What kind of people do you think they are? Take turns to say a sentence each round the class.

Ideas: talk about their hair, clothes, height, weight, personality etc.

Use: long, short, tall, small, heavy, athletic, friendly, intelligent, tidy, fun-loving, fit, easy-going etc., or choose other adjectives.

▷ *John is taller than the others.*
  Sam looks the friendliest.

3 A club for superbrains

Put the adjective in the comparative or superlative form.
Use **than** where necessary.

JENNY Have you heard of Mensa?

NICK Yes, it's the club for superbrains. I might join it.

JENNY It's ▷ *more difficult than* (difficult) you think, Nick.

You can only become a member if your IQ
is ¹_____ (high) 148.

NICK I expect mine is at least 148! Shall we do some more puzzles?

JENNY I read that Mensa already has 100,000 members, probably the
²_____ (intelligent) people in the world.
It doesn't matter how old you are.
The ³_____ (young) member is only six.

NICK Why don't you try the Mensa test?
You're ⁴_____ (good) me at school.

JENNY I don't think being ⁵_____ (clever)
someone at school also means that you are
⁶_____ (intelligent). If you are
⁷_____ (knowledgeable) someone or you
find Maths ⁸_____ (easy), you are
probably just ⁹_____ (hard-working).

NICK I'm sure you're right, Jenny.

JENNY And you are much ¹⁰_____ (quick) me
at thinking up excuses.

. . . that means my IQ is 10062.

IQ short for 'intelligence quotient'. A method of measuring intelligence. 100 is the average.

4 Work it out

a Try these puzzles.

1 Max has two boxes which together weigh eleven kilos. One box weighs ten kilos more than the other. What is the weight of each box?

Answer: Box 1 weighs _____ .

Box 2 weighs _____ .

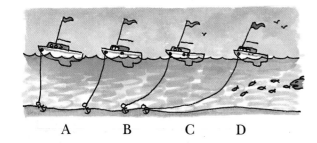

2 You want to anchor your luxury yacht. Which is the safest way to do it?

Circle the correct answer.

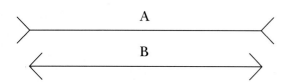

3 Which line is longer? Line A or line B?
Write the answer in a sentence.

_____ .

4 Mike is twice as old as his little sister Polly. But in five years' time, Polly will be as old as Mike is now. How old are they?

Answer: Mike is _____ .

Polly is _____ .

b Ask and answer questions round the class about the puzzles.

Use:

simple	technical	challenging
difficult	quick to solve	

▷ difficult

Which puzzle do you think is the most difficult? Do you think the first puzzle is as difficult as the fourth?

c Work with a partner. Make up a puzzle similar to one of the above puzzles. Who can invent the best one?

5 What do you think?

a Do you agree or disagree with the following statements? Put a tick in one of the boxes.

		Yes	No
1	Some people look more intelligent than others.	☐	☐
2	Girls are more hard-working than boys.	☐	☐
3	Boys are more technically-minded than girls.	☐	☐
4	Girls are better at languages than boys.	☐	☐
5	Highly intelligent people are not as practical as people of average intelligence.	☐	☐

b Choose two of the above statements and write your opinion about them in a short paragraph.

6 Class game

Take turns to say adjectives compared with **er/est** and **more/most**. You must think of an adjective within ten seconds.

If you are too slow, or make a wrong comparison, you drop out of the game.

▷ PUPIL A *hot, hotter, hottest*
   PUPIL B *comfortable, more comfortable, most comfortable*
   PUPIL C *heavy, heavier, heaviest*

11 Who are you? Adverbs of manner; Irregular adverbs etc.

Read the questionnaire, but do not answer it yet.

How ambitious are you?

Yes　No

1　Do you always take games and competitions **seriously**, even when they are just for fun?

2　Do you work **hard** at things that are important for your future?

3　Do you do things **better** when someone is watching you?

4　Do you feel **happy** if someone praises you for doing something **well**?

5　If you had organized a trip or a party for your friends very **carefully**, would you get **angry** if something went wrong?

6　In a swimming race with a friend who is younger than you, you know that you could **easily** win. Do you swim your **fastest**?

7　If you do **worse** than a friend in a school test, do you tear up your test paper **angrily**?

8　If a friend couldn't do his/her homework, would you help **willingly**?

9　Do you try to do everything as **correctly** as you can?

10　If you were ill before an exam and had **hardly** done any work for it, would you try to avoid taking the exam?

ambitious always wanting to win or be successful

Grammar lesson

Adverbs of manner

Adjectives (**serious**, **good**) tell us what someone or something is like. They describe nouns and pronouns.

Adverbs of manner (**seriously**, **well**) tell us how someone does something. They describe verbs.

> a *serious* game (adjective)
> *Do you always take games* ***seriously****?*
> (adverb of manner)

Form

We usually form an adverb of manner by adding **ly** to the adjective:

Adjective	Adverb
serious	serious**ly**
careful	careful**ly**

but **y** changes to **i** before **ly**:

easy	eas**ily**
angry	angr**ily**

and **le** changes to **ly**:

terrib**le**	terrib**ly**
simp**le**	simp**ly**

The adverb from **good** is **well**.

> a ***good*** *player* (adjective)
> BUT *Do you play* ***well****?* (adverb)

Position

Adverbs of manner usually come after the verb:

> *Do you always work* ***hard****?*

or after verb + object:

> *Do you always take games* ***seriously****?*

Adjectives instead of adverbs

The following verbs are often followed by an adjective, not by an adverb: **look**, **feel**, **taste**, **smell**; **seem**, **appear**, **become**, **get** (= become).

> *Do you feel* ***unhappy*** *if you lose?* (NOT *unhappily*)
> *Would you get* ***angry*** *if something went wrong?*
> (NOT *angrily*)

Irregular adverbs

The following words are both adjectives and adverbs: **hard**, **fast**, **late**, **straight**, **early**, **daily**, **weekly**.

> *hard* work (adjective)
> *Do you work* ***hard****?* (adverb)

Note: **hardly** means 'almost not'. Compare:

> *I work* ***hard****.* (= I work a lot.)
> *I* ***hardly*** *work.* (= I don't work much.)

Adjectives ending in **ly** usually form adverbs with the phrase 'in a way/manner'.

Adjective	Adverb
friendly	**in a friendly way/manner**
silly	**in a silly way/manner**

Also **lively**, **lovely**, **ugly**.

Comparison of adverbs

We compare adverbs ending in **ly** with **more** and **most**.

Adverb	Comparative	Superlative
eas**ily**	**more** easily	**most** easily

We compare adverbs which have the same form as adjectives, with **er**, **est**.

fast	fast**er**	fast**est**
hard	hard**er**	hard**est**
early	earl**ier**	earl**iest**

> *Do you swim your* ***fastest****?*
> *Would you work* ***harder****?*

Here are some irregular adverb comparisons.

well	**better**	**best**
badly	**worse**	**worst**
much	**more**	**most**
little	**less**	**least**
far	**further**	**furthest**

> *Do you play* ***better*** *when someone is watching?*

1 Quick quiz

Fit the adverbs from the following adjectives into the puzzle. Write the answers across.

careful   thorough   quick   easy
good   terrible   early

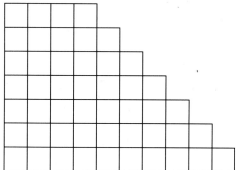

Careful, good, thorough – that's me! . . .

. . . terrible?

2 Are you ambitious?

a Do you think that you are ambitious? Write your reasons in a short paragraph. Use adverbs of manner, like this:

▷ *I think that I am quite ambitious because I try to do most things correctly.*
I don't think that I am very ambitious because I don't always try to do my best.

b Work with a partner. Ask each other the quiz questions on page 36 and tick (√) the Yes or No box. Then count the Yes answers.

If you have . . .

1 to 3:   You are not very ambitious. People like you because of this, but you shouldn't take things too lightly. Life is sometimes competitive.

4 to 6:   You are ambitious and competitive, but your ambition does not rule your life.

7 to 10:   You are too ambitious. Don't take all your activities so seriously. Try to relax and have some fun.

c With your partner write five more questions similar to the ones on page 36. Use the adverbs **badly**, **late**, **early**, **quickly** and **carefully**. Read your sentences to the class and write the best sentence for each adverb on the board.

3 All about Priscilla

Whatever Jenny's friends do, Priscilla does even better. Write the end of each sentence using the comparative form, like this:

▷ Liz speaks French quite fluently, but Priscilla _speaks French more fluently._

1   Jane swims fast, but Priscilla _____

2   Mark plays the guitar well, but Priscilla _____

3   Amanda writes neatly, but Priscilla _____

4   Marion works hard, but Priscilla _____

5   Peter learns quickly, but Priscilla _____

6   George does his homework carefully, but Priscilla _____

7   Mary can run a long way in five minutes, but Priscilla _____

8   Don arrives at school early, but Priscilla _____

9   Carol can draw animals beautifully, but Priscilla _____

10 David beats people easily at tennis, but Priscilla _____

4 Jenny's friends

Cross out the wrong word and say these sentences.

▷ Jane doesn't take games ┌ ~~serious~~/seriously ┐ .

Jane doesn't take games seriously.

1 Amanda doesn't always arrive ┌ punctual/punctually ┐ .

2 Joe always tries ┌ hard/hardly ┐ to impress.

3 Mike always plays his Walkman ┌ loud/loudly ┐ .

4 Jane sometimes spends money ┌ silly/in a silly way ┐ .

5 Don gets ┌ angry/angrily ┐ if someone cheats at cards.

6 Amanda can organize parties ┌ good/well ┐ .

7 Peter can tell ┌ funny/funnily ┐ jokes.

8 Ben sometimes behaves ┌ stupid/stupidly ┐ .

9 Liz feels ┌ unhappy/unhappily ┐

if she isn't the best in a game or quiz.

10 Marion thinks ┌ careful/carefully ┐

before she buys anything that is expensive.

Who says I don't take life seriously?

5 Write a quiz

a. Work in small groups.
Each group chooses one of the following titles
for a quiz. If you can't decide on a title, toss a
coin or choose another title of your own.

1 How brave are you?
2 How considerate are you?
3 How generous are you?

b. Discuss the meanings of the following words
and phrases in class. Suggest some more
adverbs which you could use in your quiz
questions. Write them on the board.

▷ For 1 *bravely, fast, confidently, feel/get
nervous/frightened/scared*
For 2 *willingly, quietly, in a friendly way,
patiently, feel/get angry/impatient*
For 3 *generously, willingly, voluntarily,
spontaneously, feel happy/pleased*

c. Each group now writes ten questions for the
quiz. Check the questions with the teacher
and write them on the board. Write your
questions like this:

▷ For 1 *You see a fierce-looking dog. Do you run
away as fast as you can?*
For 2 *Do you sometimes bang doors loudly?*
For 3 *Your friend has forgotten his/her snack
or lunch. Do you share your lunch with
him/her willingly?*

12 The dinosaurs are back

Adverbs of time and place;
Adverbs of degree; **too** and **enough**

NICK   Have any of you seen 'Return of the Dinos'?

BEN   Yes, I have. I saw it **at the Odeon last week.**

NICK   But you're not old **enough to** get in. You have to be fifteen.

BEN   Well, I'm nearly fifteen. I **really** enjoyed it. But it wasn't long **enough.**

NICK   Exciting films are always **too** short.

AMANDA   I liked it **very much** as well. I saw it **yesterday.** The special effects were **absolutely** great. I must admit I felt **a bit** scared when the dinosaurs started attacking people. I think the film was good **enough to** win an Oscar.

BEN   The dinosaurs looked **quite** real. I wonder if they *could* come back to life.

JENNY   Don't be silly, Ben. They died out **millions of years ago**. Some people say that the climate got **too** cold **for** them **to** live in. Others think a meteorite crashed into the Earth and made a huge cloud of dust which **completely** blocked out the sun. **Then** it got **too** dark **for** plants **to** grow.

TOM   I haven't seen the film. I got to the cinema **too** late and it had already started.

BEN   Don't worry, Tom. We'll go with you and see it again.

Oscar prize for the best film

meteorite piece of metal or stone which comes from space

Grammar lesson

Adverbs of time and place

Adverbs of time tell us *when* something happens, for example, **today**, **yesterday**, **in 1990**, **last week**, **millions of years ago**, **then**. They usually come at the end of the sentence:

*Dinosaurs died out **millions of years ago**.*

but some short adverbs (**now**, **then**, **soon**) can come at the beginning or before the main verb:

***Then** it got too dark for plants to grow.*

Adverbs of place tell us *where* something happens, for example, **here**, **there**, **at the Odeon**. They also come at the end of the sentence.

*I saw it **at the Odeon**.*

When adverbs of time and place come together, the adverb of place often comes first.

*I saw the film **at the Odeon last week**.*

In written English, adverbs of time and place often come at the beginning of the sentence.

Adverbs of degree

Adverbs of degree (**really**, **absolutely**, **completely**, **quite**, **rather** etc.) tell us *to what extent* something happens. They usually come before an adjective or adverb:

*The special effects were **absolutely** great.*
*The dinosaurs looked **quite** real.*

and before the main verb:

*I **really** enjoyed the film.*

We use **very** with an adjective or an adverb:

*The film was **very** good.*

but with a verb we use **very much** or **a lot**, not **very**:

*I enjoyed the film **very much/a lot**.*

too and enough

We put **too** before an adjective or adverb.

*Exciting films are always **too** short.*

We put **enough** after an adjective or adverb.

*The film wasn't long **enough**.*

Note the following patterns:

too/enough to + infinitive

*The film was good **enough to** win an Oscar.*

too/enough for someone **to** + infinitive

*The climate was **too** cold **for** them **to** live in.*

1 Do you remember?

Read the text again carefully, then answer the questions from memory using full sentences. Use an adverb of time, place or degree in your answers, like this:

▷ Did Ben like 'Return of the Dinos'?
Yes, he really enjoyed it.

1 Where did Ben see the film?
2 When did Ben see the film?
3 Did Ben think that the film was long enough?
4 What did Nick say about exciting films?
5 Did Amanda like the film?
6 When did Amanda see the film?
7 What did she think about the special effects?
8 How did Amanda feel when the dinosaurs started attacking people?
9 What did Amanda say about the quality of the film?
10 What did Ben say about how the dinosaurs looked?
11 When did dinosaurs die out?
12 What do some people think that a cloud of dust did?
13 What would happen if the sun was blocked out?
14 Why didn't Tom see the film?

2 Get it right!

Write correct sentences. Put the adverbs in the correct place, like this:

▷ I/at the cinema/last week/saw/a film about dinosaurs
I saw a film about dinosaurs at the cinema last week.

1 lived/about 225 million years ago/the earliest dinosaurs/on Earth

_____

2 about 65 million years ago/died out/the last dinosaurs

_____

3 in the 1820s/scientists/about dinosaurs/first learnt

_____

4 lived/on land/most dinosaurs

_____

5 in the air/flew/pterosaurs

_____

6 plesiosaurs/in the sea/swam

_____

7 were first discovered/fossils of *Tyrannosaurus*/in North America

_____

8 in the Gobi desert/in the 1920s/fossils of *Protoceratops*/discovered/people

_____

9 believe/into the Earth/a meteorite/crashed/some people

_____

10 more information/scientists/find out/every year/about dinosaurs

_____

3 It was too heavy to run

Complete the sentences with **too**, **enough**, **for** and **to**.

▷ The climate probably got ___*too*___ cold ___*for*___ the dinosaurs ___*to*___ live in.

1 After the Earth had cooled down, it wasn't warm _____ _____ the dinosaurs _____ survive.

2 Perhaps it was _____ dark _____ plants _____ grow.

3 Plant-eating dinosaurs didn't have _____ food _____ eat.

4 *Compsognathus* was only as big as a chicken. It was _____ small _____ reach the leaves on trees.

5 *Tyrannosaurus* was 14 m long, 6 m tall and weighed 7.3 tonnes. It was probably _____ heavy _____ run really fast.

6 *Tyrannosaurus* had very small hands. They weren't big _____ _____ reach its mouth.

7 Some meat-eating dinosaurs had teeth strong _____ _____ kill small animals with only one bite.

8 Scientists have found _____ dinosaur fossils _____ calculate their size and weight.

9 Some people think that some of the dinosaurs were just _____ big _____ survive on the planet.

10 No one really knows _____ about the dinosaurs _____ discover why they died out.

4 'Return of the Dinos'

a Say the sentences with the adverb in the correct place, like this:

▷ The dinosaurs looked realistic. (very)
The dinosaurs looked very realistic.

1 Amanda felt scared when the dinosaurs started attacking people. (quite)
2 Ben thought the film was exciting. (extremely)
3 They all enjoyed the film. (very much)
4 Amanda thought the special effects were good. (really)
5 Jenny thought the acting was good. (fairly)
6 They thought the idea of bringing dinosaurs back to life was clever. (rather)
7 Jane thought some of the dinosaurs looked silly. (a bit)
8 Ben thought they looked real. (quite)
9 Jenny didn't like the frightening noises. (very much)
10 On the way home they all felt nervous. (a little)

b Work with a partner. Think of a film that you have both seen. Discuss the film, then write a review of it in a short paragraph. Talk about the actors, the music and sound effects, the story, the ideas, the special effects etc. using adverbs of degree. Read your film review to the class.

▷ *We have both seen the film '. . .' We enjoyed it very much. The main actor was . . . He was extremely good.*

5 Guess the dino

a Look at the dinosaurs below and opposite. Choose one of them. Do not tell other pupils which dinosaur you have chosen. Describe the dinosaur in a short paragraph. Write about its head, neck, ears, legs, tail, feet, hands or claws. Use **quite**, **rather**, **fairly**, **very**, **extremely** etc. and suitable adjectives such as **long**, **short**, **sharp**, **small**.

▷ *Its tail was extremely long.*
Its claws were very sharp.

b Read your description to the class. The class must guess which dinosaur you have described.

14   **15**   **16**

13 From skins to jeans

Plural of nouns;
Singular and plural nouns; Possessives

Are you fashion-conscious? Do you buy new **clothes** because the length **of** the skirts or the cut **of** the trousers in your wardrobe is no longer fashionable? Are you up-to-date with **this year's** colours and styles?

From the time when **people** first covered their **bodies**, fashions have been changing. The first clothes were **animals'** skins and **leaves**. Later, people used wool from **sheep** and **hair** from goats and the use **of** woven cloth began.

Before the sixteenth century, fashion took a hundred years or more to change. It was the aristocracy who made the fashion rules. Now fashions change quickly and it's the designers in the **world's** fashion capitals who choose **this year's** colours and styles.

For centuries, western **children** from the age of three wore the same kind of clothes as their parents. **Babies** were wrapped up like parcels. As soon as they could crawl both boys and girls wore **dresses** down to their **feet**. Then they wore **men's** clothes or **women's** clothes in small sizes.

Special styles weren't made for **teenagers** until about two hundred years ago, when boys began to wear long **trousers**, blouses and caps and girls wore long dresses and straw bonnets. By the 1850s **boys'** fashions were sailor suits or knee-length trousers and jackets.

Nowadays clothes are much more practical – almost everyone has **a pair of trousers** or **jeans** and a favourite T-shirt.

Grammar lesson

Plural of nouns

	Singular	Plural
Add **s**	boy	boy**s**
	goat	goat**s**
Add **es** to **ch, o, s, sh, x**	dress	dress**es**
y after consonant → **ies**	baby	bab**ies**
	body	bod**ies**
f → **ves**	leaf	lea**ves**
Irregular plurals	child	child**ren**
	man	men
	woman	women
	person	**people**
	tooth	teeth
	foot	**feet**

Some nouns do not change in the plural.
*one sheep   three **sheep***

Singular and plural nouns

Some nouns are used differently in the singular and plural forms, for example **hair**. The hair on your head or the hair of an animal is always singular.

> *Through the centuries people have worn their **hair** in many different styles.*
> *People made clothes with the **hair** from goats.*

Separate hairs that we can count have a plural.

> *There are **two hairs** on your jacket.*

Some nouns have only a plural form, such as **clothes**, **goods**, **contents**, **surroundings**. The word **police** is always plural.

Pair nouns such as **jeans**, **trousers**, **shorts**, **pants**, **pyjamas**, **tights**, **glasses**, **scissors** are always plural. We can make them singular by adding 'a pair of'.

> ***Jeans** are always fashionable.*
> *Most young people have **a pair of jeans**.*

Some words for groups of people can be used with a singular or plural verb, for example **team**, **class**, **family**, **group**, **government**, **club**. If we think of the group as a whole we use a verb in the singular.

> *The **class likes** talking about clothes.*

Possessives

We use **'s** or **s'** with people and animals.
Singular   *a **boy's** hat   a **girl's** dress*
Plural   ***animals'** skins   **girls'** dresses*

We use **'s** with irregular plurals.

> ***men's** hats   **women's** fashions*
> ***children's** clothes*

We usually use **of** with things.

> *the style **of** clothes (NOT the clothes' style)*
> *the cut **of** the trousers*
> *the length **of** skirts*

We also use **of** with people when *who* follows.

> *What's the name **of** the woman **who** designed the mini-skirt?*

With places (**world**, **country**, **London**) we can use either the possessive **s** or **of**.

> *the **world's** fashion capitals OR*
> *the fashion capitals **of** the world*

We also use the possessive **s** with time expressions.

> ***this year's** colours and styles*
> *in **three weeks'** time*

1 Quick quiz

Fit the plurals of these words into the puzzle. Write the answers across.

leaf
sheep
child
foot
man
dress
century

2 Fashion talk

Amanda is telling Jenny about a fashion article she read in a magazine. Cross out the wrong words in the boxes.

Do you know when women first started wearing ▷ ~~x~~/– trousers? The first woman to wear [1] –/a trousers was the French actress Sarah Bernhardt.

She shocked everyone when she wore [2] a pair of/a men's trousers in 1876. She was brave enough to wear [3] it/them in public. Trousers for women [4] was/were not acceptable. It was another forty years before women dared to wear their [5] hair/hairs very short. But Annette Kellerman was even braver than Sarah Bernhardt.

Men and women used to wear swimsuits that looked like [6] –/a pyjamas, with long sleeves and long legs. In 1909 Annette wore the first swimsuit with short sleeves and she wore [7] a/– shorts ending above the knees. But the police came and [8] it/they arrested her!

3   Six hundred years of clothes

How good are you at recognizing clothes and the dates when they were worn?

a   Write about the pictures. Pay attention to singular and plural forms.

> woman/head-dress, 1450
> lady/shoe, 1900
> man/suit, 1850
> boy/suit, 1760
> girl/dress, 1810
> children/clothes, 1650
> men/shoes, 1420
> girl/bonnet, 1840
> man/hat, 1890 ✓
> women/dress, 1530

▷   man/hat, 1890

It's a man's hat from 1890.

1 _____

2 _____

3 _____

4 _____

5 _____

6 _____

7 _____

8 _____

9 _____

Check your answers with a partner, then with the teacher.

b   Work with a partner. Study the pictures and the dates for two minutes. Then cover the dates and ask each other questions about the pictures.

> ▷   PARTNER A   *Is that a man's hat from 1500?*
>   PARTNER B   *No, it isn't. It's a man's hat from 1890.*

c   How do you think fashions will look in the future? Design two articles of clothing for the year 2050 and label them as in (**a**) above. Pass your sketches round the class. Who can design the most imaginative clothes?

4 What's the name of the shop?

Complete the conversation with the possessive **s** form or **of**.

JENNY   What's the ▷ _name of the shop_ (name/shop) where you bought your new trousers?

JANE   1 _____ (Luciano/Boutique). The owner's Italian.

JENNY   Where is it?

JANE   Oh, dear. I know where it is, but I can't remember the 2 _____ (name/street). It isn't far from 3 _____ (Charly/Café). You turn right and it's at the 4 _____ (end/street).

JENNY   Well, I suppose I'll find it. What was the 5 _____ (name/assistant) who served you?

JANE   Angela. She lives next door to us. She usually works in the 6 _____ (men/department) but when it's busy she works in the 7 _____ (ladies/department) as well.

JENNY   How much were the things you bought?

JANE   I've forgotten the exact 8 _____ (price/blouse), but the trousers were £12.99.

JENNY   That's cheap. I'll go there this afternoon.

5 Clothes list

Work in two teams. Write down as many articles of clothing as you can think of in two minutes.

Write the singular and the plural form. Which team has the most correct answers?

▷ *hat, hats*
  dress, dresses
  scarf, scarves

6 Shopping

When you need new clothes, what helps you decide what to wear?

Write full sentences with **of** and say what is very/quite/not so/not at all important to you, like this:

▷ cut
  The cut of the trousers is very important.

1   price
2   colour
3   quality
4   material
5   style
6   fit
7   length
8   comfort
9   name/designer
10 size

7 Just a minute

Work in two teams. Make sure that you know the meanings of the following words/phrases and whether they are singular, plural or can be both.

scissors	hair	hairs
glasses	leaves	a pair of pyjamas
team	sheep	a pair of jeans
police	clothes	class

Choose one word/phrase and write it on a small piece of paper. Swap papers with someone from the opposite team. Do not open the paper that is passed to you until your teacher says 'Go!'

Open your papers and write a sentence of at least ten words using the word or phrase. You have only one minute to write it. The teams read out their sentences. The team with the most correct ten-word sentences are the winners.

14 Food for thought   Uncountable nouns; **some** and **any**

Nick and his friends are going hiking.

BEN   We'll need **some** maps and **some** food. I'm just making a list. We'll take **some** bread, **some** cheese and **some** bananas.

TOM   Have you got **any** drinks on your list?

BEN   Not yet. We could buy four **cartons of** orange juice.

NICK   But cartons are heavy. With **a bit of** luck we might find a mountain stream.

TOM   There may not be **any** streams. We'll have to take **some** water with us.

BEN   Shall we take **some** money, too?

JANE   There won't be **any** shops, but we'll need **some** money for the bus.

BEN   I'll finish my list now.

JANE   Would you like **some** help?

BEN   No, thanks. I'll add four large **packets of** crisps, eight large **bars of** chocolate . . .

TOM   But Ben, we're only going for one day.

hike	long walk in the country
stream	small river

Grammar lesson

Uncountable nouns

We can count nouns like **map** or **banana**. They have a singular and a plural form.

Some nouns are uncountable. They have no plural form and they take a singular verb. We use them alone or with **some/any**, **a lot of**, **not much**, **how much**. We do not use them with **a/an** or with numbers.

Kinds of food and drink (**bread, cheese, jam, milk**), materials (**wood, sand**) and abstract nouns (**luck**) are mostly uncountable. Here are some more examples.

advice	homework	news
clothing	information	progress
food	knowledge	rubbish
fun	luggage	traffic
furniture	money	weather
help	music	work

*We'll need **some food**.*
*We'll need **some money** for the bus.*

Some words which describe the weather (**rain, sunshine, snow, fog**) are also uncountable.
*There may be **some sunshine** and there won't be **any rain**.*

a bottle of/a piece of etc.

To express quantity we can make uncountable nouns countable. With kinds of food and drink we add a unit (**bar, bottle, carton, packet**) or a quantity (**kilo, litre, bit, piece, pound, slice**) + **of**.
*a **bar of** chocolate   four **cartons of** orange juice*

We can also use **a piece of** or **a bit of** with certain other uncountable nouns.
*a **piece of** advice   a **bit of** luck*

Uncountable and countable uses

Some words can be either uncountable or countable, such as **coffee, tea, ice-cream, orange juice**.
I must buy some coffee and some orange juice.
BUT *Two **coffees** and **an orange juice**, please.*
(when you order in a café)

some and any

We use **some** and **any** with plurals and with uncountable nouns.

We use **some** in affirmative sentences.
*We'll need **some** maps and **some** food.*

We use **any** in negative sentences and in most questions.
*There may not be **any** mountain streams.*
*Have you got **any** drinks on your list?*

We use **some** in questions when we expect the answer 'Yes' or when we offer something to someone.
*Shall we take **some** money?*
*Would you like **some** help?*

1 Ben's list

a Here is a list of the food that Ben wants to take with him. Complete his list with **a/an** or **some**. Write the answers.

▷ _an_	egg	▷ _some_	cheese
_____	apple	_____	meat
_____	peach	_____	sweets
_____	bread	_____	water
_____	butter	_____	biscuits
_____	tomato	_____	orange
_____	bananas	_____	crisps
_____	chocolate	_____	orange juice

b There are sixteen things on Ben's list. Read the list again, then close your books. Now tell your teacher what's on the list, using **some** or **a/an**. Write the answers on the board, then check them with Ben's list.

2 What's in the rucksacks?

a Say what the friends have got and what they haven't got in their rucksacks. Use **some** and **any**.

> ▷ *Jane has got some bread and some cheese, but she hasn't got any chocolate.*

b Work with a partner. Can you remember what's in the rucksacks? Ask and answer questions with **a packet of** etc. Use **packet**, **loaf**, **carton**, **bag**, **bottle**, **bar**, **piece**. Close your book.

> ▷ YOU   *Has Jane got a packet of crisps in her rucksack?*
> PARTNER   *Yes, she has.* OR *No, she hasn't.*

c Ask five pupils what they have got to eat in their school bags. Use **some** and **any** in the questions and answers.

> ▷ YOU   *Have you got any chewing gum?*
> PARTNER   *No, I haven't got any chewing gum but I've got some fruit.*

3 Quick thinking

a Match the pictures with the numbers. Say your answers.

1 carton
2 can
3 jar
4 tube
5 bottle
6 roll

b Make two teams. Take turns to name things that you can buy in a carton, can, jar etc. Team A gives an answer, then Team B. Score one point for each correct answer.

▷ carton
   TEAM A *A carton of cream.*
   TEAM B *A carton of yoghurt.*

4 Quick quiz

a Which words are uncountable?

Circle the uncountable words, then fit them into the puzzle. Solve the yellow word first. Here is a clue: *You don't see or hear much of it when you go hiking.*

Fit in the remaining ringed words across.

rubbish	joke	food	fun
job	lorry	luck	work
traffic	luggage	suitcase	weather

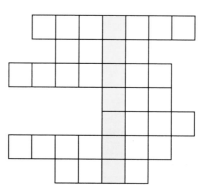

b Make sure that you know the meanings of the words in the puzzle. Write a sentence using each word. Write eight sentences altogether.

▷ fun
   We had a lot of fun last summer.

5 Preparations

Cross out the wrong words.

BEN   We need ▷ some/~~a~~ information about bus times. If we miss

the last bus home we'll have to sleep in a field.

JANE   We ought to take ¹ some/a warm clothing, just in case.

It would be ² –/a fun to sleep in a field. We could collect

³ a/some wood and make a camp fire.

NICK   Yes, and we could tell each other ghost stories. Let's

take ⁴ some/an extra food. We had better not take too

much. Walking uphill is ⁵ – /a hard work. We can't carry

⁶ any/an unnecessary luggage.

JANE   I agree. I'm going to take out my carton ⁷ of/– orange juice.

It's too heavy.

NICK   I hope we'll have ⁸ a/some good weather. Did anyone listen

to the weather forecast?

BEN   Yes, I did. There will be ⁹ some/a fog on the hills at first,

but there will be ¹⁰ a/some sunshine later.

TOM   Will there be ¹¹ a/any rain?

BEN   No rain, just ¹² a/– hurricane on the hills in the evening . . .

6 Food from A to Z

Imagine that you are going camping. Take turns
round the class to say what kinds of food you
would or wouldn't take with you. Use **some** or **any**
and a noun (plural countable or uncountable)
beginning with **a**, **b**, **c** etc. Your sentences can be
funny or serious.

▷   PUPIL A   *I would take some **apples**.*
    PUPIL B   *I wouldn't take any **butter**.*
    PUPIL C   *I wouldn't take any **cream**.*
    PUPIL D   *I would take some **dates**.*

I would take some **eggs, fish, grapes** …

Henry is **a** clerk in **an** office in town. He's also **a** health freak. He wants to live to be **a** hundred, so health is very important to him.

He gets up at five o'clock in **the** morning and lifts weights for thirty minutes. For breakfast he eats spinach and **a** raw egg with garlic and chilli pepper. It tastes disgusting, but he thinks it's good for him. Then he runs for **an** hour in **the** park, even if **the** weather is bad. He leaves for work at seven o'clock. He never goes by bus or by train and he thinks that cars are extremely dangerous. So he walks everywhere – with **a** mask over his nose and mouth. He also wears **a** uniform which he designed to protect himself from dust and dirt.

At **the** office he washes his hands ten times **a** day and he wears gloves to pick up **the** telephone in case it's dirty. He takes his lunch to work with him. He eats fifteen sunflower seeds and one onion. He is sure that **the** lunch which **the** firm provides isn't good for him.

After work he rushes home to water **the** plants. He has hundreds of plants, because they provide oxygen. In **the** evening he sometimes listens to **the** radio, but he never watches television because it might damage his eyesight.

On Monday he goes to **a** deep breathing class and on Thursday he goes to **a** vegetarian cookery class. He rarely goes to **the** cinema or to **the** theatre – there are far too many germs. He goes **to bed** early. In summer he sleeps in **a** tent in **the** garden. At **the** weekend he goes camping in **the** country, but he never sits in **the** sun. On **the** first day of every month he goes to **the** doctor's, just to make sure that he isn't ill. After all, he doesn't want to find himself **in hospital**.

> **health freak** person who thinks only of his/her health
>
> **raw** uncooked
>
> **disgusting** horrible
>
> **germs** tiny living things which can make you ill

Grammar lesson

a/an

We say **a** before a consonant sound and **an** before a vowel sound.

> *a clerk*   *a hundred*   *a uniform*
> *an office*   *an hour*

We use **a/an**

before a singular countable noun:

> *a mask*   *an egg*

before a job, a particular group of people, a nationality:

> *Henry is **a** clerk.*
> *He is **a** health freak.*
> *He is also **an** Englishman.*

in expressions with numbers when it means 'every':

> *He washes his hands ten times **a** day.*
> (ten times every day)

the

We say **the** / ðə / before a consonant sound and **the** / ðɪ / before a vowel sound.
> *the telephone*   *the evening*

We use **the** to talk about things which are clear to the listener:
> *He runs in the park.*
> (The park is close to his house.)
> *He never sits in the sun.*
> (There is only one sun.)

with some time expressions:
> *at the weekend*   *in the evening*

with dates:
> *on the first day of every month*

with some general expressions:
> *listen to the radio/news*
> *watch the news* BUT *watch television*
> *play the piano/guitar/drums*
> *go to the doctor's/dentist's*
> *go to the cinema/theatre/disco/zoo*

We do *not* use **the** with plural or uncountable nouns when we mean something in general:
> *Henry thinks that cars are very dangerous.*
> (all cars in general)
> *Health is very important to him.*
> (health in general)

with these expressions:
> *go on foot*   *go by car/bus/train/plane*

with these words when we mean **work** etc. in general:
> *at work/school/college/university*
> *go to bed/town/church/work*
> *in hospital/bed/town/prison*

(but we use **the** when we mean a particular thing: *at the office, in the town*)

in general time expressions with the names of days, months, seasons and meals:
> *on Monday*   *in June*   *in summer*
> *before breakfast*   *for lunch*

(but we use **the** when we mean a particular day/month/season/meal etc.:
> *He is sure that the lunch which the firm provides isn't good for him.*)

1 What about you?

a Not many people are like Henry. Make a list of ten differences between your lifestyle and Henry's. Take turns to read them round the class.

> ▷ *I don't lift weights before breakfast.*

b Work with a partner. Henry is giving an interview for a health magazine. Imagine that you are Henry and the interviewer. Ask and answer ten questions about Henry's routine and lifestyle. Make some notes first.

> ▷ INTERVIEWER   *What do you have for breakfast?*
> HENRY   *I always have spinach for breakfast.*
> INTERVIEWER   *What time do you go to bed?*
> HENRY   *I never go to bed later than nine o'clock.*

2 How often do you . . . ?

How many times a day/week/month/year do you do these things? Say your answers.

> ▷ wash your hands
> *I wash my hands about four times a day.*

wash your hands	travel by bus
drink a glass of milk	brush your teeth
play a sport	go to the dentist's
go shopping	go to the cinema
brush your hair	eat spinach
sleep in a tent	do the washing up
go to the doctor's	listen to the news
write a letter	use a telephone
take an exam	water the plants

I brush my hair once a …

3 More about Henry

Complete the sentences with **a/an** or **the** where necessary, like this:

▷ Henry is __a__ vegetarian, so he never eats meat. He eats strange things for ____ breakfast.

1 _____ lemons have a lot of vitamin C, so Henry eats ten _____ day.

2 Visitors to his house have to take off their shoes and leave them at _____ door.

3 Henry cleans his teeth six times _____ day.

4 For _____ supper he has a huge bowl of beans and yoghurt.

5 He believes that sitting in _____ sun even for one minute is extremely dangerous.

6 _____ health is his favourite topic of conversation.

7 On _____ Friday he goes to a Yoga class.

8 He once went to _____ cinema, but he wore his mask.

9 He is frightened of _____ hospitals.

10 He sometimes listens to _____ news on _____ radio, but it makes him nervous.

11 He is afraid that he will end up in _____ hospital.

12 He always goes to _____ bed early, even at _____ weekend.

13 He goes to _____ doctor's at least once _____ month.

14 He hates _____ buses, _____ cars and _____ planes.

15 He wears _____ gloves to open _____ doors and to pick up _____ telephone.

16 His colleagues at _____ work think that he is mad.

4 Lazy Larry

Larry is a student. He never thinks about his health. He just wants to enjoy life. Look at the pictures and write about what he does in his holidays. Make sentences using the words given. Use **a/an** and **the** where necessary.

▷ bed/ten o'clock/morning

He stays in bed until ten o'clock in the morning.

1 breakfast/four eggs/toast and jam

_____

_____

2 twelve o'clock/news/television

_____

_____

3 summer/sun/garden

_____

_____

4 afternoon/listens/rock music

_____

_____

5 evening/cinema/girlfriend

_____

_____

6 weekend/goes/cafés and discos/friends

_____

_____

7 never/bed/three o' clock/morning

_____

_____

8 takes/exercise/once/year

_____

_____

5 Your health and you

a Work with a partner. Write a questionnaire with the title 'Have you got a healthy lifestyle?' Write at least ten questions which include some of the following phrases.

for breakfast/lunch	how many . . . a day/week?
to/at school	in the morning/afternoon
in the park	to/in bed
by bicycle/bus	at the weekend
watch television	on foot
in summer/winter	take exercise

b Check your questions with the teacher. Exchange your finished questionnaire with other pupils. Ask and answer the questions with your partner.

6 Keeping fit

Write down as many ways of getting and keeping fit as you can think of in five minutes, then tell them to the class. Say when, where or how often you can do these things. Your ideas can be serious or funny, as long as they keep you fit.

▷ *You can go to a keep-fit class once or twice a week.*
▷ *You can climb the Eiffel Tower once a year.*

7 Fitness or fun?

Work in two teams. Have a class discussion. Team A argues that 'Fitness and good health are the most important things in life'. Team B argues that 'Fun and enjoyment are the most important things in life'.

First make some notes. Team A makes a statement and Team B thinks of an argument against it.

Remember that you do not use **the** when you talk about life, health, fitness, work etc. in general.

▷ TEAM A *You can't enjoy life if you aren't fit.*
   TEAM B *For most people getting fit and keeping fit is hard work. Fun is not only keeping fit. Doing lazy things is also enjoyable.*

16 The trip of a lifetime **the** with place names

AMANDA   I'd love to go to **the States**.

JENNY   You can. There's a competition in this magazine. You can win a three-week trip to **the USA** for two people.

AMANDA   Let me see. 'Visit **the White House** and climb **the Statue of Liberty!**' That sounds great. I wonder if I'll meet the President.

JENNY   Stop dreaming, Amanda. Do the competition first.

Grammar lesson

the with place names

We use **the** with the names of:

rivers	*the Mississippi*
	the River Thames
oceans, seas	*the Pacific Ocean*
	the Mediterranean
deserts	*the Sahara*
mountain ranges	*the Rocky Mountains*
island groups	*the Bahamas*
museums, galleries	*the Guggenheim Museum*
hotels	*the Sheraton (Hotel)*
cinemas	*the Odeon (Cinema)*

We do not usually use **the** with the names of:

towns, countries	*New York, America* (BUT *the USA/States, the Netherlands*)
lakes, mountains	*Lake Michigan* *Mount McKinley*
streets, squares	*Wall Street, Fifth Avenue* *Times Square* (BUT *the High Street*)
parks	*Yosemite Park* *Central Park* *Hyde Park*
shops, large stores	*Macy's, Harrods*
restaurants	*Luigi's, Joe's Snack Bar* (BUT *the Beach Café*)
airports	*Heathrow (Airport)*

With the names of buildings, bridges, monuments etc. we use **the** when the name consists of only one word:
the Capitol, the Colosseum
or when **of** is part of the name.
the Statue of Liberty
the Houses of Parliament
the Leaning Tower of Pisa

Sometimes we have to learn the names by heart because there are no rules.
the White House, the Eiffel Tower
(BUT *Big Ben, Buckingham Palace*)
the Lincoln Memorial
(BUT *Nelson's Column*)
the Golden Gate Bridge
(BUT *Brooklyn Bridge, Tower Bridge*)

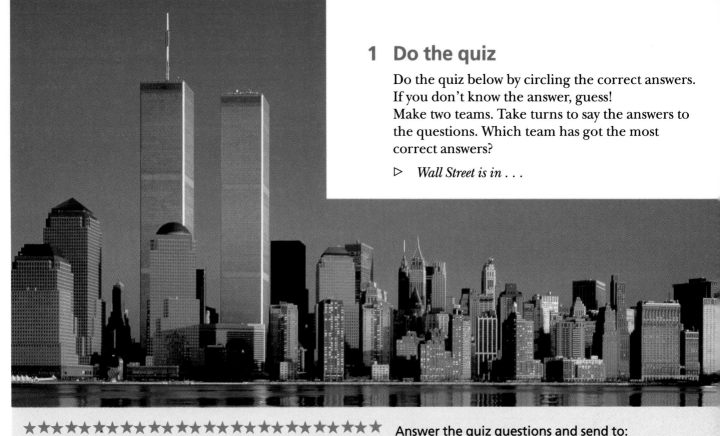

1 Do the quiz

Do the quiz below by circling the correct answers.
If you don't know the answer, guess!
Make two teams. Take turns to say the answers to
the questions. Which team has got the most
correct answers?

▷ *Wall Street is in . . .*

★Win a trip to the USA★

Answer the quiz questions and send to:
Stateside Travel
PO Box 246, London WC1

1 Where is **Wall Street**?
   a   Los Angeles
   b   Chicago
   c   New York

2 Which of these states do **the Rocky Mountains** cross?
   a   Florida
   b   Wyoming
   c   California

3 How high is **Mount McKinley**?
   a   6,194 m
   b   4,032 m
   c   7,932 m

4 In which city can you find **Brooklyn Bridge**?
   a   Chicago
   b   New York
   c   Detroit

5 Which lake is one of **the Great Lakes**?
   a   Lake Victoria
   b   Lake Michigan
   c   Lake Geneva

6 Which American state is a group of islands in **the Pacific Ocean**?
   a   Alaska
   b   Hawaii
   c   Florida

7 Where could you visit **the Guggenheim Museum**?
   a   Atlanta
   b   New York
   c   New Orleans

8 How long is **the Mississippi**?
   a   2,314 km
   b   3,799 km
   c   6,843 km

9 In which state can you find **Yosemite Park**?
   a   Ohio
   b   California
   c   Kentucky

10 In which city can you find **the Golden Gate Bridge**?
   a   San Francisco
   b   Dallas
   c   Washington

2 Where are they?

a In which cities are the following famous landmarks? Write in **the** where necessary, then write and say your answers.

Agra   Paris   Athens   Washington
Istanbul ✓   Rome   Moscow   New York
Cairo   London

▷ _____ Topkapı Palace

Topkapı Palace is in Istanbul.

1 _____ Parthenon

2 _____ Big Ben

3 _____ Sphinx

4 _____ Tower Bridge

5 _____ Eiffel Tower

6 _____ White House

7 _____ Colosseum

8 _____ Red Square

9 _____ Central Park

10 _____ Taj Mahal

b Match the pictures to the landmarks in (**a**). Say your answers, like this:

▷ *Picture 'A' is Topkapı Palace.*

B

C

D

E

F

G

H

A

I

J

K

3 What I would like to see

Write a list of ten famous places/things you would like to visit. Use **the** where necessary.

▷ *I would like to climb Mount Everest.*
   I would like to visit the Taj Mahal.

4 Sightseeing

Work with a partner. Imagine that you are going to show a pen-friend your capital city and/or the famous and beautiful things in your country. Plan a day's/week's sightseeing. When you have discussed the journey, write about it in a short paragraph. Put in **the** where necessary. Read your sightseeing tour to the class.

▷ *First we would show him/her (the) . . . After that we would go to (the) . . .*

5 Where we live

Work with a partner. Write down the names of the following. Remember to use **the** where necessary.

the cinemas/theatres in your town
the large shops or stores in your town
the restaurants in your town

the rivers and lakes in your country
the cities in your country

Exchange your lists with another pair and check the answers with the teacher. Which pair has the most correct answers?

AMANDA   Picture 4 **looks** great fun, but Picture 1 **scares** me.

TOM   I**'ve seen** bungy jumping on television. I **may** do a jump myself sometime.

JENNY   I once **read** an article about wind surfing. I **will** never do it – that's certain.

NICK   You **can** kill yourself doing sports like these. I think people who **do** them **are** crazy.

What did they say?

Amanda said that Picture 4 **looked** great fun, but Picture 1 **scared** her.

Tom said that he **had seen** bungy jumping on television and that he **might** do a jump himself sometime.

Jenny said she **had** once **read** an article about wind surfing and that she **would** never do it.

Nick said you **could** kill yourself doing sports like these. He thought people who **did** them **were** crazy.

Grammar lesson

Indirect statements in the past

When we use a reporting verb in the past (*he said*, *she told us*) to report a statement, the tense of the verb in the statement usually changes.

Direct statements		Indirect statements
present	→	past
past	→	past perfect
present perfect	→	past perfect
can	→	**could**
will	→	**would**
may	→	**might**

Amanda said, '*Picture 4 **scares** me.*' (present)
Amanda said that Picture 4 **scared** her. (past)

Jenny said, '*I once **read** an article about wind surfing.*' (past)
Jenny told us that she **had** once **read** an article about wind surfing. (past perfect)

Tom said, '*I **have seen** bungy jumping on television.*' (present perfect)
Tom said he **had seen** bungy jumping on television. (past perfect)

Jenny said, '*I **will** never go wind surfing.*' (**will**)
Jenny said that she **would** never go wind surfing. (**would**)

If a direct statement is general, or is still true when we report it, the tense does not always change.
Nick said, '*You **can** kill yourself.*' (**can**)
Nick said you **can/could** kill yourself. (**can** OR **could**)

We use a comma (,) and quotation marks (' ') in direct speech.

say and tell

Use **say** like this:
She **said**, '*I love to watch wind surfing.*'
She **said to me**, '*I love to watch wind surfing.*'
She **said** (**that**) she loved to watch wind surfing.

Use **tell** like this:
She **told me** (**that**) she loved to watch wind surfing.

See page 67 for other reporting verbs.

1 Quick quiz

Complete the sentences to solve the puzzle.

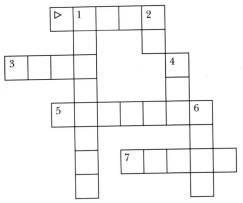

Across

▷ In indirect statements, *may* becomes _*might*_ .

3 Liz once _____, 'I like climbing.'

5 In indirect statements, the _____ becomes *past*.

7 *Will* becomes _____ in indirect statements.

Down

1 Solve 3 and 5 Across, then guess this word.

2 He said _____ me, 'Wind surfing is great.'

4 In direct statements, *could* is _____ .

6 He _____ me he might do a bungy jump.

2 Opinions

DAVID You have to be very fit to do sports like these.

MARY I don't agree. Anybody can do a bungy jump – even you.

FRANK You don't need any training for bungy jumping, but it's expensive.

ANNE I saw a television programme once about solo climbing. I think people do it just because it is exciting.

FRANK Almost anybody can go on a rafting trip – my grandfather is eighty years old and he went on one.

MARY I'll never try wind surfing. I'm afraid of drowning.

ANNE I don't think wind surfing will become very popular. Most people can't afford it.

MARY My friend started solo climbing a year ago. He fell and broke an arm once.

DAVID I have never done anything more dangerous than paddle a canoe on a lake – and even then I fell in.

paddle

canoe

What did they say? Complete with verbs in the correct tense.

David said you ▷ _had_ to be very fit to do sports like these.

Mary didn't agree. She said that anybody ▷ _could_ do a bungy jump – even David.

Frank said you ¹_____ any training for bungy jumping, but that it ²_____ expensive.

Anne said she ³_____ a television programme once about solo climbing. She thought people ⁴_____ it just because it ⁵_____ exciting.

Frank said that almost anybody ⁶_____ go on a rafting trip – his grandfather ⁷_____ eighty and he ⁸_____ on one.

Mary said she ⁹_____ never try wind surfing because she ¹⁰_____ afraid of drowning.

Anne said wind surfing ¹¹_____ become a popular sport, because most people ¹²_____ afford it.

Mary said her friend ¹³_____ his arm when solo climbing.

David said he ¹⁴_____ never done **anything more dangerous than paddle a canoe on a lake – and even then he** ¹⁵_____ in.

3 Class questionnaire

a Ask the questions round the class. Count the number of **Yes** and **No** answers and write the results in the questionnaire.

Now say the results of the questionnaire round the class.

> ▷ *Ten pupils said they enjoyed sports. Two pupils said they didn't enjoy sports.*

b Work with a partner. Write two more questions about sports like these. Ask your partner the questions. Write down what he/she said, then read it out to the class.

> ▷ I asked X, 'Which sport do you think is the most dangerous?' *X told me that he/she thought solo climbing was the most dangerous.*

Questionnaire

		Yes	No
1	Do you enjoy sports?	☐	☐
2	Which of these sports do you do?		
	a football?	☐	☐
	b swimming?	☐	☐
	c basketball?	☐	☐
3	Have you ever seen anyone doing an unusual sport?	☐	☐
4	Do you think bungy jumping is dangerous?	☐	☐
5	If you had the chance would you:		
	a do a bungy jump?	☐	☐
	b do a parachute jump?	☐	☐
	c go wind surfing?	☐	☐
6	Do you think people who do unusual sports are:		
	a crazy?	☐	☐
	b brave?	☐	☐
	c just ordinary people?	☐	☐
7	Which of the photographs on page 60 do you like best?		

1 ☐   2 ☐   3 ☐   4 ☐

4 Going solo

Read what this climber says about herself and her sport. Then write what she said.

> ▷ I am a professional solo climber.
> *She said that she was a professional solo climber.*

1 I have climbed rock faces all over the world.
2 I just use my bare hands – and my brain.
3 I have always been very fit.
4 As a child I played football and did judo.
5 I began rock-climbing in my teens.
6 I soon became addicted to it.
7 Climbing has taken over my whole life.
8 Solo climbing is very dangerous.
9 One mistake can kill you.
10 You push your body to its limits.

5 It's great fun

Nick has been talking to a girl called Kate who has done several bungy jumps. Read what Kate said.

'People often ask me what a bungy jump really is. It's very easy. All you do is jump from a bridge into a canyon with a rope round your ankles. Usually, you jump from about sixty metres. I know it sounds frightening, but it's not dangerous really. The rope can't break because it's elastic. As long as all the equipment is in good condition and there are trained people there, it's quite a safe sport. You have to be fairly fit to do a jump and you mustn't be too scared of heights!

'Most of my jumps have been in New Zealand, but I've jumped in England too. I've done twenty jumps so far. The first time I jumped I felt so scared that I almost fainted, but now I love the excitement of it. It doesn't really hurt but sometimes you feel a little bit of pain in your back when you reach the lowest point on the rope. One of the best things about bungy jumping is that you can always prove you've done a jump. Wherever you jump there is always a photographer with a video camera. You can keep the video and show it to all your friends.'

Take turns to report what Kate told Nick about bungy jumping, like this:

▷ *Kate said that you jumped from a bridge into a canyon with a rope round your ankles.*

Here are a few clues to help you:

1	height	6	numbers
2	rope	7	feeling
3	safety	8	pain
4	fitness	9	proof
5	countries		

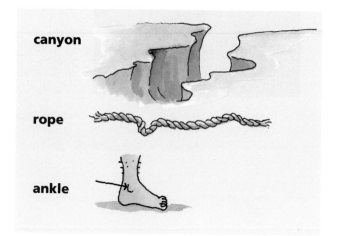

canyon

rope

ankle

6 Kangaroo jumps

Mike and Lucy have been talking about parachuting. Write what they said in direct speech, like this:

▷ Lucy said that she didn't know much about parachuting. It looked very frightening.
Lucy said, 'I don't know much about parachuting. It looks very frightening.'

1 Mike said he had been parachuting several times. It was quite frightening the first time.

2 Lucy said she had heard people talking about kangaroo jumps. She didn't understand the difference between a kangaroo jump and an ordinary parachute jump.

3 Mike said that his first jump had been a kangaroo jump. He would never forget it. Kangaroo jumps were special because you were tied to a parachuting instructor. You jumped from the plane together.

4 Lucy said that sounded less frightening than jumping alone. But she was glad she wasn't old enough to jump yet.

5 Mike said you could do a kangaroo jump when you were twelve. You could start training alone when you were sixteen, but to be an instructor you had to be nineteen.

7 Match

Match the sentence parts.

___

1

▷ Jane told Ben — 'I would like to learn how to parachute.'
Jenny told — that he wasn't afraid of heights.
Ben said — Amanda that she thought dangerous sports were stupid.
Amanda said, — that she would like to join a rafting club.

___

2

Tom said, — that he would take her rafting one day.
Jenny told — to Tom that she would go with him to the baseball match.
Amanda said — 'Basketball is better than climbing.'
Nick told Jenny — the others that climbing made her nervous.

___

3

Nick told Ben — that he had seen an exciting film about parachuting.
Jane said, — Tom that she would like to make a parachute jump.
Amanda said — 'I think rafting looks great fun.'
Jane told — to Ben that she was afraid of heights.

8 Mime game

Work with a partner. Look at the list of statements below and choose one together. Take turns to mime your situation in front of the class. (Don't speak!) When you have finished, the rest of the class must decide what you 'said', like this:

▷ I've lost my parachute.
He said that he had lost his parachute.

My bungy rope has broken.
I'm a professional tennis player.
My parachute won't open.
I'm nearly at the top of the mountain.
I want to bungy jump from the Eiffel Tower.
My canoe has capsized.
I'm a body builder.
I've lost one of my skis.
I don't want to jump from the aeroplane!
I'm a deep sea diver.

Now invent some situations of your own and take turns to mime them in front of the class.

I'm a deep-sea diver.

18 Soap operas   Indirect questions; Indirect commands, requests etc.

Here is a scene from Jenny's favourite soap opera 'Jericho Street'.

ROD   How did you find out about my letter to Caroline?

LIZ   Don't mention the letter again.

ROD   Are you still angry with me?

LIZ   Yes, and I don't want to discuss it.

ROD   Liz, give me a chance to explain – please.

LIZ   No. I won't listen to any more of your excuses.

ROD   Please don't be cross. Please . . .

LIZ   If I were you, I'd tell the truth in future.

ROD   I won't lie to you again. I promise.

What did they say?

1   Rod asked Liz **how** she **had found out** about his letter to Caroline.

2   She **told** him **not to mention** the letter again.

3   He wanted to know **if** she **was** still angry with him.

4   She said she **was** and that she **didn't want to** discuss it.

5   He **asked** her **to give** him a chance to explain.

6   She **refused to listen** to his excuses.

7   He **begged** her not **to be cross**.

8   She **advised** him **to tell** the truth in future.

9   He **promised** that he **wouldn't lie** to her again.

> **soap opera** television series shown several times a week, usually about family life

Grammar lesson

Indirect questions

In indirect questions the word order is the same as in statements. We do not use **do/does/did** to make indirect questions. We do not put a question mark at the end.

Reporting verbs for indirect questions are **ask**, **want to know**, **wonder**. The tense usually changes when we report a question. The changes are the same as in indirect statements.

If there is a question word (**who**, **when**, **why**, **how** etc.) in the direct question, we repeat it in the indirect question.

> *Rod asked Liz **how she had found out** about his letter to Caroline.*

If there is no question word in the direct question, we begin the indirect question with **if** or **whether**.

> *He asked her **if/whether** she was still angry.*

Indirect commands, requests etc.

We form indirect commands with **tell** + person + (**not**) **to** + infinitive.

> *'Don't mention the letter again,' Liz said.*
> *Liz **told** Rod **not to mention** the letter again.*

We can make indirect requests with **ask** + person + (**not**) **to** + infinitive.

> *'Give me a chance – please,' Rod asked.*
> *Rod **asked** Liz **to give** him a chance.*

Other reporting verbs can be used to report warnings, promises, offers, refusals etc. Note the structures:

beg
order
promise
warn
} someone (not) **to do** something

offer
refuse
} **to do** something

explain (to someone) that . . .
accuse someone **of doing** something
apologize for doing something
deny doing something

1 Interview with a star

TV presenter Emma Hall interviewed Don Majors, who plays Rod in 'Jericho Street'. Here is part of the interview. What did she ask him? Take turns to report the questions round the class.

▷ Don, when did you play your first TV role?
She asked him when he had played his first TV role.

1 When did you join 'Jericho Street'?
2 Do you enjoy playing the part of Rod Spencer?
3 Is it a difficult part to play?
4 How many fan letters do you get every week?
5 Has anyone ever written to you to ask you to marry them?
6 Do you think you will ever marry?
7 Are you similar to Rod in any way?
8 How many episodes of 'Jericho Street' have you made?
9 Are you planning to leave the show?
10 What do you do when fans recognize you in the street?

2 Soap opera survey

a You answered some questions for a man doing a street survey about soap operas on television. What were his questions?

Write the questions in the survey.

▷ He wanted to know if you liked soap operas.

Do you like soap operas?

1 He asked whether you watched an American soap opera called 'Manhattan'.

_____

_____

2 He wanted to know how long you had been watching it.

_____

_____

3 He asked how many of your friends or family watched it.

_____

_____

4 He asked you why it was your favourite soap opera.

_____

_____

5 He wanted to know if you would continue to watch it regularly.

_____

_____

6 He asked you who your favourite character was.

_____

_____

7 He asked you if you thought soap operas should be shown at the weekend.

_____

_____

8 He asked you if you could name four other soap operas.

_____

_____

9 He asked how long you thought a soap opera episode should last.

_____

_____

10 He wanted to know what other kinds of programme you watched.

_____

_____

b Work with a partner. Imagine that you are asking questions for the survey. Ask a partner two more questions about soap operas. Then report the questions to the class.

▷ YOU *Do you watch more than one soap opera?*

PARTNER *X asked me if I watched more than one soap opera.*

3 In the TV studio

Jim Walker, a TV director, is rehearsing a scene from a detective series called 'Inspector Thaw'. Unfortunately, he isn't very satisfied with the actors and actresses. What does he tell them to do and not to do? Say your answers.

▷ *He told Mavis not to laugh when she hit John, and to hit him harder.*

Cut!

No, no, no, Mavis. Don't laugh when you hit John. And hit him harder!

John, don't fall into the camera next time!

Don't point the gun so high, Sally, and make your hand shake more.

Read the script again, Jake. Your second line was wrong.

Tony, look more surprised when Jill enters.

Jill, remember that you are supposed to be angry. Don't smile at Tony!

And all of you, get it right this time!

Action!

4 A dream comes true

If you won a day out with a star from your favourite TV series, what would you ask him/her to do to make your day special?

Write down three things, then tell a partner what you would ask your star to do.

▷ *I would ask her to give me a signed photograph.*
▷ *I would ask him to take me to the TV studio.*

5 Accident or murder?

a Your friend missed an episode of his/her favourite series and wants to know what happened. Here is a scene from it. Write ten sentences to explain what happened.

Choose a suitable reporting verb from the box.

accuse	beg	say √
advise	deny	swear
apologize	explain	tell
ask	offer	warn √

▷ SIMON Don't go into the study, Beth. There's been a bad accident.
Simon warned Beth not to go into the study. He said that there had been a bad accident.

BETH An accident? Mike! Where's Mike?

SIMON Well, you see, he was cleaning his revolver and it just went off. Please, please believe me . . .

BETH No! I don't believe you! You killed him!

SIMON No, Beth. I didn't. I swear that I'm telling the truth.

BETH I'm sorry I accused you, Simon. It's a terrible shock.

SIMON You'd better sit down. I'll get you a glass of water. The police will be here soon.

b Work with a partner. Look at the scene carefully. Do you think Simon was telling the truth? What do you think might have happened? Discuss your opinions with the class.

6 Write your own soap opera

Work with a partner. Invent two characters and give them names. Write a scene with at least six sentences. It can be funny or serious. Your characters should ask, tell, advise, warn, accuse, offer etc.

a. Write what each character says (direct speech). It will help if you read again what Simon and Beth say in Exercise 5.
b. Together, read (or act!) your scene to the class.
c. Pupils take turns to report the scene with **ask, tell, advise, warn** etc.

NICK   What are you reading, Jenny?

JENNY   I'm reading a book about handwriting. Did you know that **your** handwriting can tell you about **your** character?

NICK   No, I didn't. What does the book say about **my** handwriting?

JENNY   **Yours** is bigger than **mine**. Big writing means that you are friendly, optimistic and ambitious. Look, here are some examples of signatures. **This** one here shows that the writer is sporty because there are lots of loops in it. **That** one at the bottom is very neat. It means that the writer is calm and affectionate.

These three are examples of very small writing, which means that you can concentrate well and are modest. **Those** on the next page are examples of big writing, which means that you are ambitious and not very tactful.

NICK   **This** is fun. What about Tom's writing? **His** has big spaces between all the words.

JENNY   **That** means that he is careful and likes being alone.

NICK   And Amanda's? **Hers** has small spaces between the words. And what about **our** teachers' writing? They are always complaining about pupils' handwriting, but **theirs** is sometimes worse than **ours**.

---

signature eg. *J Watson*
loop eg. *l*
affectionate *loving*
modest *not wanting to show that you are good/clever at something*

Grammar lesson

Demonstratives

Singular	**this**	**this** writing
	that	**that** writing
Plural	**these**	**these** signatures
	those	**those** signatures

We usually use **this/these** for things that are close in space or time. **here** often follows.
> *This signature here shows that the writer is sporty.*
> *This is fun.*

We usually use **that/those** for things that are further away in space or time. **there** or an expression of place often follows.
> *That one at the bottom is very neat.*

Note that we often use **one** after **this/that** instead of repeating the noun.

We also use **that/those** to compare or contrast two or more things which are close to us. We use **this/these** for the first thing, then **that/those** for other things in the comparison.
> *This signature shows that the writer is sporty.*
> *That one means that you are calm and affectionate.*
> *These three are examples of small writing.*
> *Those are examples of big writing.*

Possessive adjectives and pronouns

Adjectives	Pronouns
my	mine
your	yours
his	his
her	hers
our	ours
your	yours
their	theirs

A noun follows a possessive adjective but not a possessive pronoun.
> *That's **my handwriting**.* OR *That's **mine**.*
> *It's **her signature**.* OR *It's **hers**.*

1 Is this right?

Write in **this**, **that**, **these** or **those**.

Please find enclosed before we send the tomorrow morning

she lets Ben do anything he wants

▷ _This_____ writing is neat, but _that_____ writing looks untidy.

Jenny Castle   *A HCmm*

1 I can read _____ signature here, but I can't read _____ one at all.

isn't the only way forward. There must

far too many however we

2 _____ letters are small, but _____ letters are large.

telling myself that is all the

not able and with hens, eggs and all

3 _____ large loops mean that you are thoughtful and imaginative. _____ pointed loops mean that you are curious and critical.

Before we go. Bye bye,   *Birthday card*

4 _____ capital B is narrow. It means that you are shy. _____ capital B shows intelligence and clear thinking, because it's simple.

we will keep on looking for the

A lot of other things can happen

5 The spaces between _____ words are wider than the spaces between _____ words.

2 His or hers?

Write in the missing words, **my**, **mine**, **your**, **yours** etc.

▷ 'Is that your writing?' 'Yes, it's _mine_____ .'

1 'Is that Jenny's writing?' 'No, _____ is smaller.'

2 Let's compare _____ writing. Is yours as big as _____ ?

3 'Is that Tom's signature?' 'I don't know. It could be _____ .'

4 Your capital letters are taller than Jane's but _____ small letters are bigger than _____ .

5 'Is that your signature?' 'No, it isn't _____ .'

6 Our teachers complain about bad writing, but sometimes we can't read _____ .

7 My writing means that I can concentrate well. What does _____ mean?

8 If you don't close _____ O's and A's, it means that you are talkative.

9 You can find out about your friends' characters by studying _____ handwriting.

10 'You can write much faster than me.' 'But _____ writing isn't as neat as _____ .'

3 Compare your writing

Work in groups. Write three sentences on a piece of paper and compare your handwriting with your partners'. Find as many differences and similarities as you can. Tell the class. Say sentences with **my**, **mine**, **her**, **hers**, **his** and **our**.

▷ *His writing is bigger than mine.*
My capital letters are smaller than hers.
Our loops on 'g' and 'y' are similar

Tom and Nick want to go camping in Wales during the holidays. They need to buy a tent and some pieces of equipment before they go. They also have to pay their train fare to Wales.

NICK The cheapest tent we have seen costs £55. We haven't got **much** money so we both need to start saving our pocket money.

TOM You're right. I get £5 every fortnight and I usually only buy **a few** magazines. I should be able to save about £4 of it.

NICK That's great. I get **a little** more than you because I do **a lot of** extra jobs for my Mum and Dad. I should be able to save as **much** as £7 a fortnight.

TOM I wonder if I could get more pocket money if I did **a few** more things at home.

NICK There's **little** hope of that, Tom! You don't like working. How **much** do we need altogether?

TOM Well, the tent is £55, the train fare is £10 each and we need **a little** spending money as well as **a few** things to cook with. We need to save about £50 each.

NICK It will be quite hard but I think we'll manage it. How **many** weeks are there before the school holidays?

TOM Nine, I think. That gives us quite **a lot of** time, doesn't it?

NICK Yes, it does, and if you do **a few** jobs at home, we'll save a lot of money!

Grammar lesson

a lot of

We use **a lot of** (or **lots of**) with plural and uncountable nouns in affirmative sentences.
*I do **a lot of/lots of** extra jobs for my parents.*
*That's quite **a lot of time**.*

We can use **a lot** without a noun.
*That's quite **a lot**.*

much, many

In questions and in negative sentences **much** and **many** are usual.

We use **much** with uncountable nouns.
*How **much** money do we need?*
*We haven't got **much** money at the moment.*

We use **many** with plural nouns.
*How **many** weeks are there until the school holidays?*

a little

We use **a little** with uncountable nouns. It has a positive meaning. It means 'a small amount'.
*I get **a little** more than you.*

little (without **a**) has the negative meaning 'not much, nearly no'.
*There's **little** chance of that!*

a few

We use **a few** with plural nouns. It has the positive meaning 'a small number'.
*I usually buy **a few** magazines.*

few (without **a**) has the negative meaning 'not many, nearly no'.
***Few** parents give their children more than five pounds a fortnight.*

Comparisons

a lot	more	most
little	less	least
few	fewer	fewest

*Tom gets **less** pocket money than Nick.*

1 They'll have to save

Complete with **a lot of**, **much** or **many**.
Sometimes more than one answer is possible.

▷ Nick and Tom have _a lot of_ saving to do
before they can go camping.

1 Neither Tom nor Nick has _____ money.

2 The boys haven't got very _____ time
before the school holidays start.

3 If they both do _____ jobs at home they
should have enough.

4 The train fares won't cost _____.

5 Nick wants to take as _____ tins of food
and packets of biscuits as possible.

6 _____ of the things they need are quite
expensive.

7 They won't need to take _____ spending
money.

8 Tom wants to buy _____ books and
magazines to read on the train.

9 Tom doesn't usually do _____ work at
home, but now he'll have to.

10 The boys haven't been on _____ camping
holidays, so they need lots of equipment.

2 What do they spend money on?

a In Britain, most young teenagers spend their money on
magazines, music, sport and entertainment, clothes
and sweets.

Work with a partner. Look at the pie charts below
and talk about the information using **more**, **less**, **fewer**
and **not as much/many**, like this:

▷ *Girls spend less money on entertainment than boys.* OR
Girls don't spend as much money on sport as boys.

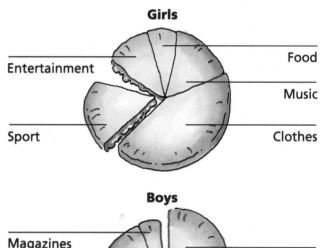
Girls

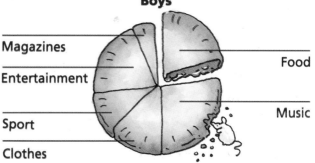
Boys

b Think about how you spend your money. Find four
things that you both spend money on, for example,
magazines or sweets. Draw a pie chart each to show
how much money you spend and what you spend it on.

Compare your pie chart with your partner's.
Write some notes first, then tell the class the results.
Use **more**, **less**, **fewer** and **not as much/many**, as in (**a**),
like this:

▷ *I buy fewer comics than X.*
X doesn't buy as many sweets as I do.

3 Don'ts from A to Z

Say what you don't usually buy with your pocket
money.

Try to use **not many/much** . . . alternately and a
word beginning with **a**, **b**, **c** etc. It can be serious
or funny. If you can't think of a noun, use an
adjective. Here are some suggestions:

▷ *I don't buy many **apples**, **aeroplanes**.*
*I don't buy much **bread**, **banana** ice-cream.*
*I don't buy many **comics**, **chickens**, **cups**.*
*I don't buy much **dog** food . . .*

21 Missing   something, nobody, everywhere, anyone etc.

Do you believe that there are people who can 'see' what is happening **somewhere else**? Gerard Croiset from Holland could and he used his unusual ability to help the police to find missing people, **anywhere** in the world.

Professor Sandelius lived with his 24-year-old daughter Carol in Topeka, in the USA. One day, **something strange** happened. Carol disappeared. The police looked for her **everywhere**. First they showed photographs to **everybody** in town, but **nobody** knew **anything** about her. Then they started a nationwide search, but they couldn't find her **anywhere**. After eight weeks there was **nothing else** that the police could do.

Professor Sandelius was prepared to try **anything** to find his daughter. He had heard about Croiset and he contacted him. 'Can you do **something** to help?' he asked. '**No one else** can.'

Croiset never refused to help people. He told Professor Sandelius that Carol was alive. 'I see her **somewhere** near water and small boats. Now I see her riding with **someone** in a lorry and now in a big red car. Don't worry. You will know **something** definite in six days.'

Five days passed and Professor Sandelius still hadn't heard **anything**. On the sixth day, early in the morning, he went downstairs to telephone Croiset. He was amazed to see that **someone** was sitting on the sofa. It was his daughter, safe and well!

The details which Croiset had given were accurate. He had 'seen' Carol from 8,000 kilometres away. He had told the police where she was, and they had brought her home.

Gerard Croiset died in 1980. He never took money for his detective work.

Grammar lesson

something, nobody, everywhere, anyone etc.

things	something	anything	everything	nothing
people	somebody	anybody	everybody	nobody
	someone	anyone	everyone	no one
places	somewhere	anywhere	everywhere	nowhere

somebody and **someone**, **nobody** and **no one** etc. mean the same.

We use **some-**, **every-** and **no-** in affirmative sentences.
   *The police looked for her **everywhere**.*   ***Someone** was sitting on the sofa.*

We usually use **any-** in questions and in negative sentences.
   *The police couldn't find her **anywhere**.*

We can use **some-** in questions when we expect the answer 'Yes'.
   *Can you do **something** to help?*

We can use **any-** in affirmative sentences with the meaning 'every-' for emphasis.
   *He was prepared to try **anything** to find his daughter.*
   *He helped the police to find missing people, **anywhere** in the world.*

We can use **else** after all the words with **some-**, **any-**, **every-** and **no-** with the meaning 'other' or 'different'.
   no one else = 'no other person'
   somewhere else = 'a different/another place'

We can use an adjective after words with **some-**, **any-** and **no-**.
   something strange, something definite, nothing new

What shall I tell this man? I can't see **anything**.

1 She was safe and well

Write in the correct missing word. Choose from **something**, **someone**, **anything**, **everything**, **everyone**, **nothing** or **no one**, like this:

▷ Sandelius thought that _Something_ terrible had happened to his daughter Carol.

1 He asked _____ he knew if they had seen her.

2 The police did _____ possible to find Carol.

3 They started by showing _____ photos of Carol.

4 _____ had seen Carol.

5 After eight weeks the police still couldn't tell him _____ new.

6 There was _____ else they could do.

7 He was sure that there must be _____ that _____ could do.

8 He phoned Gerard Croiset and told him _____ .

9 Croiset had the ability to 'see' _____ .

10 Carol was safe and well. _____ terrible had happened to her.

2 On the telephone

a Work with a partner. Take the roles of Sandelius and Croiset. Write the next part of their telephone conversation. Do not change the facts, but use your imagination for the details.

Use **something**, **nobody**, **everywhere** etc. at least six times. Write the scene like this:

▷ SANDELIUS *Something terrible has happened. I need your help. My daughter is missing and nobody can find her . . .*

CROISET *Tell me something about your daughter.*

b Check what you have written with the teacher. Then learn it and act it to the class.

3 Are you a good detective?

A pupil leaves the room. The class chooses an object in the room which everybody can see. When the pupil comes into the room, he/she must guess the object by asking questions with **anywhere**. The class answers in full sentences with **somewhere** and **nowhere**.

▷ PUPIL *Is it anywhere near the window?*
CLASS *No, it's nowhere near the window.*
PUPIL *Is it anywhere on the floor?*
CLASS *Yes, it's somewhere on the floor . . .*

4 Lost and found

When was the last time that you lost something important, for example, keys, a purse, a camera, tickets, a pet etc?

Write some notes first, then talk for two minutes about it. Say what you lost, where you looked, who you asked, how you found the missing object etc. Use **something**, **someone**, **somewhere** etc. If you have never lost anything, invent a story.

▷ *About a year ago I lost my keys. There was **nobody** at home so I couldn't get in. I looked for them in my pockets, in my schoolbag, **everywhere** . . .*

5 Something else

Pupil A says a phrase with **else**, for example **something else**, **nobody else**, **everywhere else**. Then Pupil A names another pupil who has to say a correct sentence within ten seconds, using the phrase. If Pupil B can't, Pupil A must say a sentence.

▷ PUPIL A *My phrase is 'everything else'. George.*
GEORGE *There's only an apple in the fridge. I've eaten **everything else**.*

both, neither, either; all, none; would prefer to, would rather

Maria, Ivanka and Albert are **all** extremely rich – and they **all** wish they could play in a park, but **none** of them can.

Maria Dupré and Ivanka Perez are **both** daughters of industrialists. They **both** wear dresses which cost thousands of dollars, but **neither of them** has ever been shopping alone. **Neither** child has ever been anywhere without her bodyguards. Albert's father is dead. He was a prince. Now Albert von Blankheim lives in a huge castle in Germany, with his mother and his bodyguards. The ten-year-old **would rather** play in a public park **than** in his castle garden. He **would prefer to** go to school **rather than** study at home. But he isn't allowed to do **either**.

All of the children have villas, yachts and huge bank accounts, but **none of them** has a real friend.

---

bodyguard someone who is paid to protect a rich or famous person

public open for everybody, not private

Grammar lesson

both, neither, either

We use **both**, **neither** and **either** to talk about only two people or things.

both takes a plural affirmative verb. It goes after **be** and before full verbs. It means 'the one and the other'.

> They are **both** daughters of industrialists.
> They **both** wear dresses which cost thousands of dollars.
> **Both of them** have huge bank accounts.

neither usually takes a singular affirmative verb. It usually goes at the beginning of the sentence. It means 'not the one and not the other'.

> **Neither of them** has ever been shopping alone.
> **Neither** child has ever been anywhere without a bodyguard.

either after **not** means the same as **neither**.

> He is **not** allowed to do **either**.

all, none

We use **all** and **none** to talk about more than two people or things.

all takes a plural verb. It goes after **be** or before a full verb.

> They are **all** extremely rich.
> They **all** wish they could play in a park.
> **All of them** have villas and yachts.

none usually takes a singular verb, but a plural verb is also possible. **none** usually goes at the beginning of a sentence.

> **None of them** has/have a real friend.

would prefer to, would rather

would prefer (not) to and **would rather (not)** mean the same. To compare things, we use **(rather) than**.

> He **would prefer to** go to school **rather than** study at home.
> He **would rather** play in a public park **than** in his castle garden.

1 Maria and Ivanka

Put in **both of them** or **neither of them**. Write your answers.

▷ _Both of them_ are daughters of wealthy industrialists.

1 _____ go anywhere alone.

2 _____ have long, blonde hair.

3 _____ have private hairdressers.

4 _____ wear dresses which cost thousands of dollars.

5 _____ has ever been in a department store.

6 _____ likes eating lobster or caviar.

7 _____ have over a hundred pairs of shoes.

8 _____ needs pocket money.

9 _____ has ever played in a park.

10 _____ would love to go to a cinema.

2 Maria, Ivanka and Albert

Is it **all** of them or **none** of them? Tick your answers, like this:

All   None

▷ ☑ ☐ of them are in danger of being kidnapped.

1 ☐ ☐ of them knows what it is to save money.

2 ☐ ☐ of them wear designer clothes which cost thousands of dollars.

3 ☐ ☐ of them have several bodyguards.

4 ☐ ☐ of them has ever been in a bus.

5 ☐ ☐ of them are driven everywhere by chauffeurs.

6 ☐ ☐ of them stay at home.

7 ☐ ☐ of them has ever made a friend of their choice.

8 ☐ ☐ of them hate photographers.

9 ☐ ☐ of them have servants and private teachers.

10 ☐ ☐ of them will ever go to a rock concert.

3 Imagine!

Work with a partner. Think of five things you like about Maria, Ivanka and Albert's lives and five things you don't like. Tell the class what you think. Use 'We both' or 'Neither of us', like this:

▷ *We both think that wearing expensive clothes must be nice. Neither of us thinks that it is fun to have bodyguards.*

4 I'd rather do it my way

Imagine that you are the son or daughter of very rich and famous parents. Describe your life and what you would like to change about it.

Use **would rather do** and **would prefer to do**. Write a short paragraph, then read it to the class.

▷ *I have to wear designer clothes, but I'd rather wear old jeans and T-shirts.*

I'm very happy wearing designer clothes.

23 Faraway faces

so and **such (a)**; **every** and **each**; **one(s)** for substitution

NICK I'm reading a book about Easter Island. It's **so** far away from any other country **that** few people have visited it. It's 3,860 kilometres from Chile. Have you heard of it?

TOM Yes, I have. Why do people say it's **so** mysterious?

NICK Well, there are hundreds of huge stone statues around the coast of the island and **each of them** weighs up to eighty tonnes. Almost **every** statue has its back to the sea.

TOM Why are the statues **so** big? And why are there **such** a lot of them?

NICK No one really knows. Some of the statues have got **such** long ears, too. This book says there were two different races of people on the island and **each** race built statues. The short-eared **ones** were built first. Look. Here's a picture of **the ones** with long ears. And look at **this one** with the huge hat on its head. Take the book, Tom. Perhaps you can solve the mystery.

Grammar lesson

so and such (a)

We use **so** with an adjective alone.
> Why are the statues **so big**?

We use **such** with a noun (with or without an adjective before it).
> Why do they have **such long ears**?
> It's **such** a mystery.

Compare:
> The story is **so strange**.
> It's **such a strange story**.

Note also:
so far, such a long way
so much/many, such a lot (of)

After **so** and **such (a)** we can use **that** to show result.
> Easter Island is **so far away that** few people have visited it.

every and each

We use **every** and **each** before a noun in the singular.

Sometimes we can use **every** or **each** without a difference of meaning,
every/each week/day/morning/time

We use **every** to talk about the things or persons in a group *together, as a whole*. **almost**, **nearly** and **not** can come before **every**, but not before **each**.
Almost every statue has its back to the sea.
Not every statue has a hat.

We use **each** to talk about the things or people in a group *separately*.
There were two races of people and each race built statues.

We can use **of** after **each**, but not after **every**.
Each of them weighs several tonnes.

one(s) for substitution

We use **one** or **ones** instead of a countable noun to avoid repetition. **one**(s) always comes after an adjective or **the**.
There are statues with long ears and with short ears. The short-eared ones (= statues) were built first.
Here's a picture of the ones with long ears.

We can also use **one**(s) after **this**, **that**, **these**, **those**, **which** and **other**.
Look at this one with the enormous hat.

1 Unanswered questions

a You are asking an expert on the history of Easter Island the following questions. Complete them with **so** or **such** (**a**), like this:

▷ Why did the inhabitants of Easter Island make ___*such*___ huge statues?

1 Why do the statues have _____ big heads?

2 Why are the statues _____ similar?

3 Why was the place where the statues stand _____ long way from the place where they were made?

4 The statues are _____ heavy. How were the islanders able to transport them twenty kilometres across the island?

5 How were the islanders able to lift _____ heavy weights without machines?

6 Why did the islanders stop making the statues _____ suddenly?

7 Why are _____ many unfinished statues lying face downwards in a huge pile?

8 How could the islanders have had _____ good tools with which to carve the statues?

9 Why did the islanders build _____ many statues?

10 Why did the islanders consider the statues to be _____ important?

b Now imagine that you are the expert on Easter Island. Discuss possible answers to the questions in (**a**) in class. Use your imagination. No one knows the real answers.

▷ *Perhaps they built such huge statues so that they could be seen from every point of the island.*

2 Such a strange island

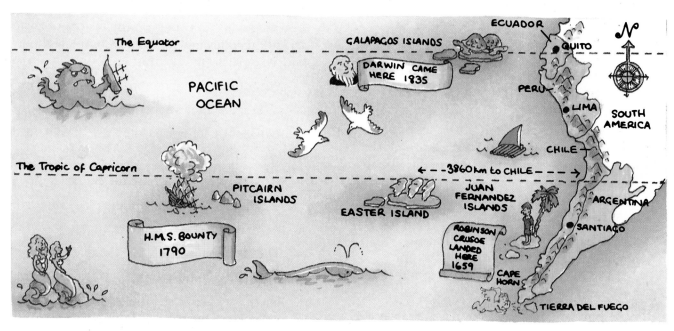

Rewrite the sentences with **so** or **such** (**a**) so that the meaning is the same, like this:

▷ Easter Island is so far away from Chile.
  (Easter Island . . .)
  *Easter Island is such a long way
  from Chile.*

1 It is such a small island that hardly anyone
  knows it. (The island . . .)

  _____

  _____

2 It is so far to Pitcairn Island, where the nearest
  people live. (It is . . .)

  _____

  _____

3 There are so many strange stone statues on
  Easter Island. (There are . . .)

  _____

  _____

4 Their ears are so long. (They have . . .)

  _____

  _____

5 They have such short necks. (Their necks . . .)

  _____

  _____

6 Their chins are so pointed. (They have . . .)

  _____

  _____

7 The island is so mysterious. (It is . . .)

  _____

  _____

8 The statues have such interesting faces.
  (Their faces . . .)

  _____

  _____

9 There are such a lot of questions without
  answers. (There are . . .)

  _____

  _____

10 So many people have tried to solve the mystery
  of Easter Island. (Such . . .)

  _____

  _____

3 Easter Island facts

Complete with **each** or **every**. Write both if you think that both words are possible.

▷ There are over 600 statues on Easter Island and ___each___ of them is at least ten metres high.

1 _____ of the statues looks inland.

2 _____ statue has a huge head.

3 Almost _____ statue is carved out of one piece of stone.

4 Not _____ statue has a hat.

5 There were two races on the island. _____ race created a different kind of statue.

6 Boats come to the island to bring food and supplies, but not _____ week.

7 Not _____ statue has long ears.

8 _____ statue must have taken years to build.

9 Nearly _____ year someone tries to solve the Easter Island mystery.

10 _____ of the statues is important to the people of Easter Island.

4 The Bermuda Triangle

Work with a partner. Take the parts of Nick and Jane. Which words can you replace with **one** or **ones**? Circle the words first, then read the conversation, replacing the words. When you think you've got it right, read the conversation to the class.

NICK I've got a lot of books about mysteries.

JANE Have you got any really good ▷ (books?)

NICK Well, how about this book? It's about the Bermuda Triangle. The other books aren't as exciting.

JANE That's the place where boats and planes disappear, isn't it?

NICK Yes, hundreds of boats have disappeared, not only small boats but large boats, too. And aeroplanes. I've read all the stories. There are some very exciting stories.

JANE What about the theories which try to explain the disappearances? Which theory do you believe?

NICK The most popular theory says that magnetic forces send ships off course in storms. But the theory that I like most says that the disappearances are caused by a strange force unknown to science.

JANE Do you really believe that?

NICK Yes, why not? Do you see that picture?

JANE Which picture?

NICK The picture of the yacht.

JANE Which yacht?

NICK The yacht on the right at the top. It disappeared without trace on the way from Nassau to Miami in 1974. And look at those planes, the planes on page 62. All five simply disappeared over the Bermuda Triangle in 1945. That's very strange.

theory idea which explains why something happens

5 Choices

Work with a partner. Look at the pictures. Take turns to ask your partner the questions. Give answers using **one** or **ones**.

▷ YOU   *Which T-shirt would you buy?*
   PARTNER   *I'd buy the one with the triangles on it.*

1 Which dog would you like to own?
2 Which car would you like to drive?
3 Which hotel would you like to stay in?
4 Which watch would you like to have?
5 Which boat would you like to sail in?

Reflexive and emphatic pronouns;
each other, one another;
have/get something **done**

Imagine **yourself** at sea in a small boat – alone. You are sailing round the world. There is no one to talk to except **yourself** and a goat. You and the goat have little to say to **each other**. He refuses to behave **himself**. He has eaten your maps for breakfast, your straw hat for supper, a rope and a piece of sail. He is always getting **himself** into trouble. You wish you could just throw him into the sea, but you are a patient man. You are also a clever sailor. You can even make your boat steer **itself** when you want to sleep.

It is a hundred years ago and you are Joshua Slocum, the American who was the first man to sail round the world by **himself**. He was very poor and could not **get** a boat **built** for his journey. 'I found an old fishing boat rotting in a field,' he said. 'I said to **myself**, "This will do fine." So I bought it and rebuilt it, using wood from an oak tree which I cut down **myself**.'

Sailing **by yourself** for months is hard. When you need to **have** your hair **cut**, or to **have** a sail **mended**, there is no one to do the job for you. You have to do everything **yourself**. When there are strong winds and waves as tall as a house, only you can save **yourself** from drowning.

Since Slocum's day several people have sailed round the world by **themselves**. They have radios to entertain **themselves** and they and their families at home can talk to **one another**. If they get into difficulties they can have **themselves** rescued by other ships or helicopters.

Grammar lesson

Reflexive and emphatic pronouns

Pronouns	Reflexive/Emphatic pronouns
I	**myself**
you	**yourself**
he	**himself**
she	**herself**
it	**itself**
we	**ourselves**
you	**yourselves**
they	**themselves**
one	**oneself**

We use a reflexive pronoun after a verb when the subject and the object are the same person.
*I said to **myself**, 'This will do fine.'*
*Imagine **yourself** at sea in a small boat.*

We often use reflexive pronouns after **behave, burn, cut, defend, enjoy, help, hurt, introduce, kill, look at, talk to, teach**.
*The goat refuses to behave **himself**.*

We use **myself** etc. for emphasis. An emphatic pronoun can mean 'without help'. It usually comes at the end of the sentence.
*Slocum said, 'I cut down the tree **myself**.'*

by myself etc. means 'alone'.
*Sailing **by yourself** for months is hard.*

each other, one another

We use **each other** and **one another** with two or more people. They have the same meaning.

*You and the goat have little to say to **each other**.*
(= You have little to say to the goat and the goat has little to say to you.)
*They and their families can talk to **one another**.*
(= They can talk to their families and their families can talk to them.)

have/get something done

We use **have** + object + past participle to say that somebody does a job for us.

*When you need to **have** your **hair cut**, there is no one to do the job for you.*

Be careful with the word order. Compare:

*I **had** my hair **cut**.*
(= past simple. The hairdresser cut it.)
*I **had cut** my hair.*
(= past perfect. I cut my hair myself.)

Sometimes **get** is used instead of **have**.

*He couldn't **get** a boat **built** for his journey.*

1 Round the world

Complete the sentences with **myself, yourself** etc.

▷ Slocum rebuilt his boat *himself* .

1 He used wood from an oak tree. He said, 'I cut the tree down _____ .'

2 Slocum was the first person to sail round the world by _____ .

3 At sea, Slocum talked either to the goat or to _____ .

4 When Slocum was asleep, his boat steered _____ .

5 The goat was always in trouble. He refused to behave _____ .

6 Slocum visited many islands. On Robinson Crusoe's island he taught people how to make doughnuts. When he left they could make them _____ .

7 Slocum's journey was very adventurous. During his trip he had to defend _____ against pirates three times.

8 Since Slocum's day, many people have sailed round the world by _____ .

9 The Australian May Cottee was one of the first women to sail round the world by _____ .

10 When you are alone at sea, you have to do everything _____ .

2 Atlantic crossing

Work with a partner. Imagine that you have just crossed the Atlantic together.

Write a short paragraph about your trip, using some or all of these words with **each other** or **one another**: know, like, talk to, help, argue, blame, annoy, rely on, be proud of, like this:

▷ *My friend and I have known **each other** for six years. During our trip we sometimes argued with **one another**, but . . .*

3 Home again

When Joshua Slocum returned to America after three years at sea, he probably had the following things done. Say your answers.

▷ *He had his beard shaved off.*

Relative pronouns

Bob Geldof is an Irish pop musician who has raised a lot of money for charity.

Geldof, **whose** mother died when he was young, came from a very poor family. He was born in Ireland. After he had left school he lived in England, then in Vancouver in Canada, **where** he wrote about pop music for a magazine. Back in his home town of Dublin, he and some **friends he had known** since childhood formed a successful pop group called 'The Boomtown Rats'. In 1984, Bob saw a film of a famine **that** was devastating Ethiopia. He had the idea of producing a record **which** could be sold to help the famine victims. The song 'Feed the World' raised £8 million. It was sung by an all-star rock group **which** Geldof called 'Band Aid'.

In July 1985, Geldof organized a huge charity pop concert for television, **which** was watched by one and a half billion people. **The £70 million the concert raised** helped hungry people all over the world. On the day of the concert Bob Geldof said, 'I think this must be the greatest day of my life.'

---

raise money collect money

charity 1 help for the poor
2 organization which raises money for the poor

famine a great lack of food

devastate destroy, ruin

aid help (often money, food, medical supplies)

a billion one thousand million (1,000,000,000)

Grammar lesson

Relative pronouns

We introduce relative clauses with the relative pronouns **who**, **which**, **that**, **whose** and **where**.

We use **who** for people and **which** for things. We can also use **that** for both people and things, but **who** is more usual for people.

> *Bob Geldof is a musician **who** is famous for helping to raise money for charity.*
> *He organized 'Live Aid', **which** was watched by millions of people all over the world.*
> *He saw television pictures of a famine **that** was devastating Ethiopia.*

When **who**/**which**/**that** is the object of the relative clause, we can leave it out.
> ***some friends he had known** since childhood*
> (OR ***some friends who/that he had known***)

To show possession we use **whose**.
> *Geldof, **whose** mother died when he was young, came from a very poor family.*

We can use **where** to talk about a place.
> *He lived in Vancouver, **where** he wrote about pop music for a magazine.*

1 Singing for others

a Complete with **who** or **which**.

▷ Bob Geldof is a singer and songwriter
  _____who_____ was born in Ireland in 1954.

1 He is the famous pop musician _____ organized charity pop concerts in the 1980s.

2 'I don't like Mondays' is the name of one of his songs _____ became a big hit.

3 'Feed the World' is the song _____ raised £8 million for famine relief in Ethiopia.

4 'Band Aid' was the name of the group _____ sang the number one hit.

5 Geldof travelled all over the world. He found a lot of famous people _____ were willing to give money for his projects.

b Write in **who** and **which** only if they are necessary.

1 Before Bob became a pop star, he had many

   different jobs _____ he didn't like.

2 Being a music journalist in Canada was a job

   _____ he enjoyed.

3 'The Boomtown Rats' is the name of the group

   _____ he formed in Dublin.

4 Geldof wrote a best-selling book about his life

   _____ is called *Is that It?*

5 People _____ know Geldof say that he

   is a very kind person.

2 Mother Teresa

Put in **who**, **which**, **whose** or **where**. If **who** and
which are not necessary, don't write them.

▷ Mother Teresa is a name _____

   everybody knows.

1 Mother Teresa, _____ real name is

   Agnes Bojaxhiu, was born in 1910.

2 Mother Teresa is a missionary _____

   has helped sick people all over the world.

3 Agnes, _____ father was a grocer,

   decided to become a nun at the age of twelve.

4 Her father, _____ came from Albania,

   supported her decision.

5 Teresa is the name _____ she took

   when she became a nun at the age of twelve.

6 In 1928 she went to India _____ she

   taught in Calcutta.

7 She looked after poor people _____

   lived on the streets.

8 She says, 'Being unwanted is the worst disease

   _____ a person can have.'

9 India, Africa, America and Australia are

   countries _____ she has opened

   homes, schools and hospitals.

10 In 1979 she won the Nobel Peace Prize

   _____ made her world-famous.

3 Interview

Find someone who . . .

can name two charities
collects money for a charity
owns a T-shirt from a charity
sometimes gives pocket money to a charity
has done something special to raise money

Go round the class asking your questions.

▷ *Can you name two charities?*

Write down the names of the pupils who give you a
Yes answer. The first person to get five Yes answers
is the winner. Report your answers to the class.

▷ *I have found someone who . . . It's X.*

4 Write a quiz

Work in small groups.

How many charities can you think of that raise
money to help national and international
organizations? How many famous people can you
think of who have helped to raise money for
charities?

Make quiz questions for the class, like this:

▷ *What is the name of the charity which . . .*
▷ *What is the name of the famous person who . . .*

5 Discussion time

Do you agree or disagree with this statement?

'People who are born rich should help people who
are born poor.'

Think of reasons for and against giving money to
charities. Then write your opinion in a short
paragraph.

I'm a famous person who helps.

Mary Anning was a palaeontologist, the name for someone **who studies fossils**. Lyme Regis, **where Mary lived all her life**, is famous for its fossils. Mary's father, **who was a carpenter**, collected them and sold them. They brought in money **with which he improved his small income**.

Mary loved the beach they went **to** and she soon learned to recognize the fossils her father was looking **for**. She continued to collect fossils after he had died. One day she discovered something **that looked like the head of a large crocodile**. Using a hammer and a chisel, she broke away the rock and underneath it she found an ichthyosaurus. She sold it for £23. In 1824 she discovered a complete plesiosaurus, **which died over 50 million years ago**. This time it was the Duke of Buckingham **to whom** she sold it, for £157. Mary became famous throughout the country.

> **fossil** remains of animal or plant which died long ago, now hard like rock
>
> **carpenter** a person who makes things from wood
>
> **income** money you earn for work you do

ichthyosaurus

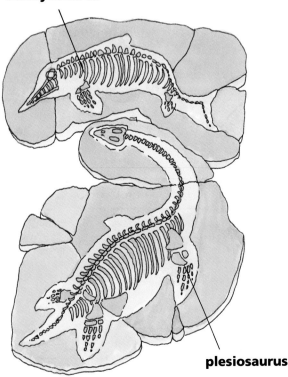

plesiosaurus

Grammar lesson

Relative clauses

Defining relative clauses

Defining relative clauses are necessary for the meaning of the sentence. We do not separate them with commas from the rest of the sentence.

> *Mary was a palaeontologist, the name for someone **who studies fossils**.*
> *Mary discovered something **that looked like the head of a large crocodile**.*

Non-defining relative clauses

Some relative clauses give extra information which is not necessary for the meaning of the sentence.

> *Lyme Regis, **where Mary lived all her life**, is famous for fossils.*
> *Mary's father, **who was a carpenter**, sold them.*

We call them non-defining relative clauses. They:

are separated by commas
are not introduced by **that**
do not leave out **who** or **which**
are typical of written English
are often found in news reports

Prepositions in relative clauses

In spoken English, prepositions usually go at the end of a relative clause.

> *the fossils (which/that) he was looking **for***
> *the beach (which/that) they went **to***

In written English the preposition can go at the beginning of the clause. **Who** becomes **whom** when we use a preposition before it.

> *They brought in money **with which** he improved his small income.*
> *It was the Duke of Buckingham **to whom** she sold the plesiosaurus.*

1 All about Mary

Join the two sentences together using **who**, **which** or **whose**. Sometimes the relative clause goes in the middle, sometimes at the end.

▷ Mary's father collected fossils.
He was a carpenter.

Mary's father, who was a
carpenter, collected fossils.

1 The Annings lived in Lyme Regis.
It is on the south coast.

_____

_____

2 Mary had a younger brother.
He was called Joseph.

_____

_____

3 Lyme Regis is famous for fossils.
They can be found in the white cliffs.

_____

_____

4 Mary found an ichthyosaurus.
She was fascinated by fossils.

_____

_____

5 She also discovered a plesiosaurus.
It died 50 million years ago.

_____

_____

6 The Duke of Buckingham bought the huge fossil for £157. He was a very rich man.

_____

_____

7 Mary also found lots of smaller fossils.
They were bought by museums throughout the world.

_____

_____

8 Mary was visited by the King of Saxony.
Mary was very famous.

_____

_____

2 Life in Lyme Regis

Say the sentences, putting the preposition at the end.

▷ Lyme Regis is the town in which Mary lived.
Lyme Regis is the town the Annings lived in.

1 It is also the town in which she was born.
2 The Anning children loved the beach to which they used to go.
3 The study of fossils was something about which Mary knew a lot.
4 It was a subject in which she and her father were very interested.
5 It was the Duke of Buckingham to whom Mary sold the plesiosaurus.
6 It was Mary to whom the King of Saxony paid a visit.
7 It was Mary from whom famous collectors bought fossils.
8 Many people visited the museums in which her fossils were kept.

3 Class game

a Match the pictures with the descriptions below.

▷ you cut things with it
a knife (f)

1 you measure temperature with it
2 you chop wood with it
3 you can ride on it
4 you look through it
5 you can sleep in it
6 you take photographs with it

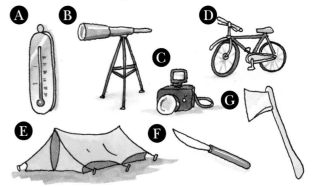

b Choose one of the objects for the class to guess. Write a sentence to describe it, putting the preposition at the end. The class asks questions about the object, like this:

▷ a knife
CLASS   *Is it something you cut things with?*
PUPIL   *Yes, it is.* OR *No, it isn't.*

27 Survival in the jungle   Ability

Jungles are full of fierce animals. No human **could** survive in one for very long. They **wouldn't be able to** find food or shelter. However, here are two stories which prove that people **can** survive in the jungle for a long time.

The ape child

In 1965, a strange creature was found in the jungles of Sabah in South East Asia. It was a little boy who behaved like an ape. Nobody **could** understand how such a strange creature **had managed to** survive in the jungle. Scientists carried out some tests and discovered that the boy had been looked after by orang-utans. They gave him a nickname: Simboy. The orang-utans had looked after him very well. Simboy **had been able to** find nuts and fruit. He **could** climb tall trees and he **could** run much faster than an ordinary human. Simboy **couldn't** speak. He just made strange noises. He **wasn't able to** walk like a human: he **could** only run by using his arms as well as his legs.

The Peruvian plane crash

In 1992, three Americans were flying over Peru in a small aeroplane. Suddenly the engine failed and the plane crashed in the middle of the jungle. At first, the pilot thought he **could** prevent the plane from bursting into flames. He was wrong. The fuel tank was on fire. The three friends **managed to** get out of the plane seconds before it exploded. Unfortunately they hadn't taken any food with them and they **couldn't** radio for help because all their equipment had been destroyed by the fire. All they **could** do was hope that someone would find them. They **managed to** find a river and so they **were able to** drink. They lived on water and fruit for twenty-eight days. Finally, a helicopter team **managed to** rescue them. It was lucky that they **had been able to** find enough food to survive for so long.

> **prevent** stop something from happening
>
> **survive** continue to live
>
> **shelter** a place where you are protected from danger or bad weather

Grammar lesson

Ability

Present

We use **can** and **cannot** (**can't**) for ability in the present.

*The stories prove that people **can** survive in jungles.*

We can use **am/are/is able to** instead of **can**, but **can** is more usual.

Past

We use **could** for general ability in the past and usually before **see**, **hear**, **smell**, **taste**, **feel**, **remember**, **understand**.

*Simboy **could** climb tall trees.*
*Nobody **could** understand how he had managed to survive.*

could not (**couldn't**) is used in general and in particular situations.

*Simboy **couldn't** speak.*

We use **was/were able to** for ability in a particular situation in the past.

*They found a river and so they **were able** to drink water.*

If the action was especially difficult, we can use **managed to** instead of **was/were able to**.

*The three friends **managed to** get out of the plane.*

Other uses of **be able to** and **could**

We use **be able to** to form other tenses and after **will**, **would**, **should**, **must**, **may**, **might** etc.

*They were lucky that they **had been able to** find enough food to survive for so long.*
*They **wouldn't be able to** find food or shelter.*

could can also mean 'would be able to'.

*The pilot thought he **could** prevent the plane from bursting into flames.*

1 How to survive

a If you were lost in a jungle, you would have to be able to do certain things in order to survive. What five things can you already do that would help you if you were alone in the jungle? Say your answers, like this:

▷ *I can swim underwater, but I can't hold my breath underwater for very long.*

Here are some ideas to help you:

climb trees	swing on a rope
run very fast	make a fire
use a compass	recognize poisonous plants
build a shelter	make a rope ladder

b Work with a partner. Ask and answer questions with **could** about the activities in (**a**).

▷ PARTNER A *Could you climb trees when you were eight ?*
 PARTNER B *Yes, I could, but I couldn't swim underwater.*

Imagine that you are going on a survival training course. Say what you **will be able to do** after the course. Use the activities in (**a**) or your own ideas. Say five sentences.

▷ *After the course I will be able to find my way by reading the stars.*

2 Lost in Peru

a Complete the sentences with **couldn't** or **was able to**.

Petra was flying a helicopter over the Peruvian jungle when suddenly there was a huge storm. She ▷ *couldn't* bring the helicopter under control and seconds later the helicopter crashed to the ground.

Petra fell 5,000 metres. Luckily, she was still strapped to her seat. That is how she 1_____ survive the fall. Rescue parties searched the jungle for several days, but they 2_____ find either Petra or the helicopter. Even radar equipment 3_____ find her. The jungle was so dense that the rescuers 4_____ see through the trees.

Petra knew that she 5_____ survive for long without water. She 6_____ find a river because she had been on a survival training course. She realized that she 7_____ defend herself against wild animals, so she built a shelter. At first Petra 8_____ find any food that was safe to eat. She had studied botany at University, so she 9_____ recognize the poisonous plants. She 10_____ find enough to eat for several days at a time.

b Work with a partner. In a short paragraph, write what you think happened to Petra next. Use **couldn't**, **was able to** and **managed to**, like this:

> ▷ *Petra was bitten by a dangerous insect. She was very ill and she couldn't move for two days. She was hungry and exhausted. Luckily she managed to find some plants and some fruit to eat. When she felt better she decided to light a large fire. Petra was able to send smoke signals and finally . . .*

c Take turns to read your paragraph to the class.

3 Gold!

Work in groups. Fifty years ago a plane carrying gold crashed in the Brazilian jungle. No one has found it yet. You are near the area where the plane crashed. You are going to camp in the area and look for the gold.

Draw an imaginary map of the area, showing mountains, rivers, jungle paths, the nearest villages or towns etc. Mark the place where you plan to build your camp.

a You can take five pieces of equipment and five items of food with you. Choose the ten things. Write them down in sentences, giving reasons for taking them, like this:

▷ *We are taking a hammer so that we can build a tree house.*
▷ *We are taking some tinned food because we won't be able to survive on fruit.*

b Now write a paragraph explaining the whole plan. Remember the jungle is full of fierce wild animals, poisonous snakes etc. Use **can**, **can't**, **will/won't be able to** etc.

Read your plan to the class, like this:

▷ *We are building our camp at the top of a tall tree. Our camp will have three ropes so that we can swing down to the ground. We are taking some bottles of water because we may not be able to find fresh water . . .*

4 A lucky escape

Think of an accident that once happened to you or to someone you know. If you can't think of a true story, invent one. Use **couldn't**, **was able to**, **managed to**. Write your story first, then read it to the class, like this:

▷ *When I was five I fell into a river. I couldn't swim. I shouted as loudly as I could and a fisherman heard me. The fisherman jumped into the water and managed to pull me out.*

5 Guessing game

Work as a class. Make a list of ten objects that would be useful or necessary in a jungle, for example: a knife, a box of matches, a sleeping bag. One pupil leaves the room. The class chooses one object from the list. When the pupil returns he/she must guess the object by asking only three questions with **Can you . . . ?**

▷ PUPIL *Can you cut things with it?*
CLASS *Yes, you can.* OR *No, you can't.*

One day, while they were playing in the sand near their home in New Zealand, nine-year-old Patrick and two friends found a giant egg. It was over a hundred times bigger than a chicken's egg. '**Can** we keep it?' Patrick asked. 'Of course you **can**,' said his father. Patrick's friend added, 'I once found some old coins and I **was allowed to** keep them.' The children wanted to know all about their egg, so they wrote a letter to a scientific laboratory. This is what they said.

'**Could** you please help us to find out about our egg? **May** we bring it to show you? **Would** you please do some tests and tell us what's inside it? **Are** children **allowed to** visit your laboratory? If they are, **could** we please come soon?'

Patrick and his friends **were allowed to** take their egg for laboratory tests. The tests showed that it was an egg of the extinct elephant bird and that it was at least two thousand years old. What a surprise! 'We **will be allowed to** keep it, won't we, Dad?' Patrick asked.

The children and their egg soon became famous. They appeared on television and someone offered them 75,000 dollars for it. They began to plan how they would spend the money. But it was all too good to be true. One day, a government letter arrived which said:

'The egg is public property. You **are not allowed to** keep things which belong to the State. We are sorry but you will have to give the egg to us. We will pay you some money, but only a small amount.'

'They **can't** have it!' said Patrick. 'If we **can't** have it, nobody **can**.' Patrick was very angry. He buried the egg in the sand again and he still refuses to tell anyone where it is.

Grammar lesson

Requests

We use **could you** or **would you** when we ask someone to do something. They are more polite than **can**.

> *Could you please help?*
> *Would you please do some tests?*

Permission

We use **can**, **could** or **may** to ask for permission. **could** is more polite than **can**.

> *Can we keep it?* (Patrick asks his father.)
> *Could we come soon?*
> (Patrick is more polite in his letter.)

may is more polite than **can** and **could**.

> *May we bring it to show you?*

We use **can** to give permission.

> *Can we keep it?*   *Of course you can.*

We use **can't** to refuse permission.

> *'They **can't** have it!' said Patrick.*

We often use **be allowed to** to ask for, give or refuse *official* permission, which has to do with rules and regulations.

> *You **are not allowed to** keep things which belong to the State.*
> *Are children **allowed to** visit your laboratory?*

We often use **be allowed to** for permission in the future and in the past.

> *We **will be allowed to** keep it, won't we?*
> *I once found some old coins and I **was allowed to** keep them.*

1 Could you please . . . ?

When Patrick and his friends took their egg to the laboratory, they asked a scientist to find out lots of things.

a Make their requests with **Could you** . . . ? Say your answers.

▷ They asked the scientist to tell them how old the egg was.
Could you please tell us how old the egg is?

1 They asked the scientist to find out what was inside.
2 They wanted the scientist to explain the tests to them.
3 They wanted the scientist to tell them what kind of egg it was.
4 They asked the scientist to find out what the eggshell was made of.
5 They wanted the scientist to tell them all about the elephant bird.

b Now make the requests again, with **Would you** . . . ?

c With a partner, write five more requests which you would have made if you had found the egg. Use **could** and **would**.

2 Asking permission

a Patrick and his friends asked for permission to do the following things in the laboratory. Ask their questions using **can** or **may**.

▷ They wanted to look through the microscopes.
Can/May we look through the microscopes?

1 They wanted to look at the equipment.
2 Patrick wanted to help with the tests.
3 They wanted to stay until the tests were over.
4 Patrick wanted to see the results on the computer screen.
5 They wanted to take the results home.

b Work with a partner. One partner is Patrick, the other partner is the scientist. Ask for permission to do the things in (**a**). Give or refuse permission with **can**, **can't** or **be allowed to**.

▷ PATRICK   *Can/May I look through the microscopes?*
SCIENTIST   *Yes, you can.* OR *No, I'm sorry you can't. Children aren't allowed to use the equipment.*

3 Write a letter

Work with a partner. Imagine that you want to visit a museum with your class. Write a polite letter to the museum director. In your letter, make requests and ask permission to do the following things, or make your own requests.

You want to see a special collection or department – for example, the dinosaurs.

You want permission to take photographs.

You want the director to arrange a museum tour with a guide for two hours.

You want to know the cost of the tour for a group of thirty pupils.

You want to make the visit without a teacher.

You would like to take food and drinks with you.

4 Are you allowed to . . . ?

What are you allowed to do where? Say what you think.

▷ in a cinema
stand up during the film/eat and drink/smoke?
You aren't allowed to stand up during the film. You are allowed to eat and drink if you don't make a noise. You aren't allowed to smoke.

1 in a library
talk loudly/run about/sit and read?
2 on a plane
play a radio/open the door/talk to the pilot?
3 in a museum
take photographs/touch things/talk to the museum attendants?
4 in a public park
pick the flowers/play football/drop litter?
5 at school
eat during lessons/listen to music/shout?

29 A purse full of pounds Possibility; Deduction

Jack is on his way to the sports centre to meet some friends. He's feeling miserable because he hasn't got any money. It's his girlfriend's birthday next week. He **may not** be able to buy her a present and she **could** be very disappointed. She **might** even refuse to go out with him! He **could** ask a friend to lend him a few pounds, but he already owes money to all his friends.

When he arrives at the sports centre, he sees something pink near the entrance. It's a purse and it's full of money. Fifty pounds! Who **could** it belong to?

'A pink purse **can't** belong to a boy. It **must** belong to a girl at the centre,' Jack thinks.

Jack doesn't know what to do. He **could** pay his debts with the money and he **could** buy Debbie a present. There's no one in the street, but someone **might** be watching him.

---

debt money that you owe

Grammar lesson

Possibility

We use **may** or **might** to talk about something that is possible or probable now or in the future.

*His girlfriend **may** be very disappointed.*
(= Perhaps she will be very disappointed.)
*She **might** even refuse to go out with him.*
(= She will probably refuse.)

The negative forms are **may not** (no short form) and **might not** (**mightn't**).

*He **may not** be able to buy his girlfriend a present.*
(= Perhaps he will not be able to buy a present.)

We also use **could** for possibility in the future.

*He **could** pay his debts with the money.*
(= It would be possible for him to pay his debts.)

Deduction

We use **must** to say what is logically certain in a situation. We make a deduction from the facts.

*It **must** belong to a girl at the centre.*

We use **can't** for the negative.

*A pink purse **can't** belong to a boy.*

1 Perhaps . . .

Rewrite the sentences with **may**.

▷   Perhaps the purse belongs to a girl at the centre.
    The purse may belong to a girl at the centre.

1   Perhaps the owner is looking for the purse.
2   Perhaps Jack knows the girl.
3   Perhaps someone will be watching Jack.
4   Perhaps he won't tell anyone about the purse.
5   Perhaps he won't try to find the owner.
6   Perhaps he will put the purse back where it was.
7   Perhaps he will find the owner.
8   Perhaps Jack will get a reward for finding the purse.

2 Probably . . .

Say what might happen. Say what you think Jack might or might not do.

Tell the class your ideas. If the class thinks that your idea is probable, write your sentence on the board.

▷ *Someone might ask him if he has found a purse.*
▷ *He might not keep the money.*

3 What could he do?

a What could Jack do with the money?
Write five sentences.

▷ *He could pay his debts.*

b What else could Jack do to get money?
Say sentences round the class.

▷ *He could do a few jobs at home.*

c Say what you could do with fifty pounds in your currency. Think of five things.

▷ *I could buy some new clothes.*

4 Making deductions

Complete the sentences with **must** or **can't**.

▷ It's an expensive leather purse. It isn't scratched. It ___*must*___ be quite new.

1 It still smells of leather, so it _____ be very old.

2 Jack thinks, 'The owner _____ get a lot of pocket money.'

3 Why does Jack think that the purse _____ belong to a girl?

4 Why _____ it belong to a boy?

5 The owner _____ be very careless to lose so much money.

6 The owner _____ know that she has lost the purse outside. No one is looking for it.

7 It _____ be a shock to lose so much money.

8 It _____ be wonderful to find so much money!

5 Whose is it?

a Imagine that you have found these things in the street or on a bus. Make deductions about the things or the owners with **must** and with **can't** (where possible). Say your answers.

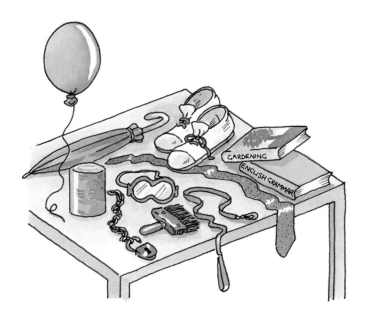

▷ a dog's lead
It must belong to someone who has a dog.
The owner must have a dog.

a pink umbrella	a pair of football boots
a paintbrush	an English grammar book
a bicycle lock	a balloon on a string
a tin of cat food	a mask
a silk tie	a book about gardening

b A pupil thinks of one of the above objects. The class asks questions and tries to guess the object. The pupil answers with **Yes, you can/No, it isn't** etc. After an answer the class says a sentence with **It could be/It can't be** or **It must be**.

▷ CLASS *Can you use it in the rain?*
PUPIL *No, you can't.*
CLASS *It can't be the umbrella. Can you read it?*
PUPIL *Yes, you can.*

BEN   I'd like to go on a TV game show. What do you **have to** do to become a game show contestant?

NICK   I expect you **have to** send a photograph and tell them about yourself.

BEN   What do you think they look for when they choose people?

NICK   It probably depends on the kind of game show. You **mustn't** be shy or nervous. You **needn't** be very clever, but you **have to** be able to react quickly or be good with words.

BEN   **Do** you **have to** be over a certain age?

NICK   You **have to** be over twelve for 'Let's Go', but for 'Risk It' you **mustn't** be over fifteen.

BEN   Well, I **must** get my hair cut so that I'll look good in my photograph.

> **contestant** someone who takes part in a game or competition

Grammar lesson

must, have to

We use **must** or **have to** for necessity in the present.

Use **must** if *you* think something is necessary.
> *I **must** get my hair cut.*

Use **have to** if *others* say that something is necessary, or to talk about official rules or general regulations.
> *You **have to** be over twelve for 'Let's Go'.*
> *What do you **have to** do to become a game show contestant?*

We use **had to** for the past and **will have to** for the future.

mustn't, needn't, don't have to

We use **mustn't** to say what is not allowed or not advisable. **mustn't** is stronger than **shouldn't**.
> *You **mustn't** be over fifteen.* (not allowed)
> *You **mustn't** be shy or nervous.* (not advisable)

We use **needn't** or **don't have to** to say it is not necessary to do or be something.
> *You **needn't/don't have to** be very clever.*

1 Rules of the game

Put in **have to** or **mustn't**.

Here is some advice on being a good game show contestant.

▷ First, you _have to_ choose the quiz or game show that's right for you.

1 If you are unfit, you _____ apply for a show with a lot of action.

2 You _____ apply many months before the show.

3 You _____ send a photograph and fill in some forms.

4 You _____ tell lies on the forms and you _____ send a photograph of someone else!

5 In most game shows you _____ think quickly or you _____ run around the studio and do funny things.

6 If you don't win you _____ cry or throw things at the presenter.

7 You _____ be a good loser.

8 You _____ behave as if you are better than the other contestants.

9 If you win a prize, you _____ look disappointed if you don't like it.

10 You _____ be fair and accept rules and decisions.

2 Take your chance

a Work with a partner. A television company has chosen you to invent a new game show. It will be shown on television once a week. It must be suitable for teenagers. Write a short letter to the television company explaining how your show will work. Use **have to**, **must, mustn't** and **needn't**, like this:

▷ *The show is called 'Take your chance'. You must be between 13 and 16 years old. You have to play in two teams. You mustn't be unfit because you have to climb ropes and do a lot of running. Each team must have four players. They needn't be very good at sports but they must be fun-loving . . .*

b The class is the board of managers of the television company. They ask questions about your show using **Do you have to?**

▷ *Do you have to be talkative?*
Do you have to be very muscular?

3 Who am I?

In this game show, mystery celebrities tell the audience facts about themselves. The audience has to guess the mystery celebrity's name by asking him/her questions with **have to**.
The celebrity can only answer using **must**, **mustn't** and **needn't**, like this:

▷ CELEBRITY *I **needn't** be very fit to do my job, but I **must** enjoy being outdoors.*
AUDIENCE *Do you **have to** work alone, or with someone else?*
CELEBRITY *I usually work with a group of people, but I **needn't** be with them all the time.*
AUDIENCE *Do you **have to** use any special equipment?*
CELEBRITY *I travel a lot, often on foot, so I **mustn't** take anything too heavy. I **must** have a very good camera.*
AUDIENCE *Are you David McGregor, the famous wildlife photographer?*

Now play the game. Pupils take turns to be the mystery celebrity and the class asks questions.

NICK   There's a science competition in this magazine. It says you can work in pairs or groups and it can be on any topic you like. **Shall we** enter it?

TOM   Yes, **let's** do a project on the solar system. **We could** get some books out of the library and start doing it now. What **shall I** do first?

NICK   Write a list of things to do. **Why don't we** write to the Young Scientists' Society and ask if they can send us some posters and information?

TOM   That's a good idea. **Shall I** write the letter? Then **I could** make a model of the solar system and draw a map to show how far the planets are from the Sun.

NICK   Yes, and while you do that **I'll** go and get some big sheets of paper. **I can** write fact sheets about each of the nine major planets. I already know that the solar system measures over 12,000 million kilometres across and I know quite a lot about the planets, moons and comets that travel around the Sun. **Would you like** me to borrow some of my father's books, so that we can find out more about the smaller planets?

TOM   That would be good. We need as much information as possible. **Can I** do anything else? **Shall I** write something about the size of the Sun? Did you know that the Earth would fit inside its volume over a million times?

NICK   No, I didn't. **Let's** start work. I think we're going to win this competition.

Grammar lesson

Offers

When we offer to do something, we use **shall**, **will/'ll**, **can** or **would like**.

Shall I write the letter (for you)?
I'll go and get some big sheets of paper.
Can I do anything else?
Would you like me to borrow some of my father's books?

Suggestions

To make a suggestion, we use **let**, **shall**, **can/could** or **why don't**.

Let's start work.
Shall we enter it?
I can write fact sheets about the planets.
We could get some books out of the library.
Why don't we write to the Young Scientists' Society?

To ask for a suggestion, we use **shall**.

What shall I do first?

1 Can I help?

Ben needs something to do. He is offering help to the others. Write two sentences that you think he might say. Use **Shall I . . . ?** and **I'll . . .** , like this:

▷ Nick's computer won't work.
  Shall I try to mend it for you?
  I'll lend you my computer.

1 Tom needs some books from the library but he's lost his library card.

_____

_____

2 Nick can't find the address of the Young Scientists' Society.

_____

_____

3 Nick hasn't got enough money to buy the sheets of paper he needs.

_____

_____

4 Nick's father can't remember where he put his books on the planets.

_____

_____

5 Tom needs some coloured pens to draw the planets with.

_____

_____

6 Tom doesn't know how to spell some of the names of the planets.

_____

_____

7 Nick needs some change for the telephone.

_____

_____

8 Tom has lost his new telescope.

_____

_____

9 Nick hasn't got a stamp for the letter to the Young Scientists' Society.

_____

_____

10 Tom wants to find out about Mars.

_____

_____

2 What shall I do?

Work with a partner. Think of five problems each and write them on pieces of paper. If you can't think of real problems, invent some. Swap pieces of paper and take turns to give each other advice using **why don't you . . . ?** and **you could . . .** , like this:

▷ PARTNER A   *I've got a flat tyre and I need to go into town.*
   PARTNER B   *Why don't you pump it up?* OR *You could take the bus into town.*

3 Making a documentary

Work in small groups. You have been asked to make a ten-part documentary about space.

Discuss the kind of documentary you want to make. Take turns to make suggestions to your group. When you all agree, write down the best suggestions. Use **shall we**, **let's** and **we can/could**, like this:

▷ *Shall we make the first one about the Moon?*
▷ *Let's have one programme on space travel and UFOs.*
▷ *We could show some satellite pictures of Mars.*

32 I'm not a child   ought to, should; had better; be supposed to

JANE   Sylvia is having trouble with her parents. They say she **ought to** do more at school. She knows she **should** work harder for the exams, but she's angry because her parents don't like her friends. Although she's almost sixteen, she'**s supposed to** be home every night by eight o'clock.

NICK   Perhaps her parents **ought to** trust her more. They **shouldn't** treat her like a child. Why don't they like her friends?

JANE   I'm not sure. Sylvia's mother says that they are very rude. They don't do any school work. Sylvia **is supposed to** do her homework every night but she goes out with her friends instead. She says she wants to leave home.

NICK   She **had better not** do that. She might regret it.

JANE   But her parents just complain and never listen.

NICK   I think they **had better** start listening before it's too late.

Grammar lesson

ought to, should

We use **ought to** and **should** to give general advice or say what we think is right. They have the same meaning. In question and negative forms we use **should** more than **ought to**.

> She **ought to** work harder.
> They **shouldn't** treat her like a child.

had better

We also use **had better** to give advice. 'You had better . . .' means 'It would be better if you . . .'

> They **had better** start listening before it's too late.
> She **had better not** do that.

The short form is **'d better (not)**.

be supposed to

We use **be supposed to** to talk about something that is expected, because someone has ordered or arranged it.

We also use **be supposed to** to say what someone should do but doesn't do.

> Sylvia **is supposed to** be at home by eight o'clock.
> (Her parents have ordered her to do this.)
> She **is supposed to** do her homework.
> (but she doesn't)

---

1 What do you think?

What do you think Sylvia, her parents and her friends should do to improve the situation?

a   Say sentences from the table.

> ▷ *Sylvia should/ought to talk to her parents.*

Sylvia	should	talk to her parents.
Her parents	shouldn't	work harder.
Her friends	ought to	listen to Sylvia.
		leave home.
		leave school.
		be more tolerant.
		be rude to her parents.
		ask her friends home.
		be so strict.
		trust Sylvia.
		encourage Sylvia to leave home.

b   What else do you think Sylvia, her friends and Sylvia's parents ought to/should or shouldn't do? Write five more suggestions. Take turns to read them to the class.

> ▷ *Sylvia's parents should try to get to know her friends better.*

3 What are you supposed to do?

a Sylvia is supposed to be home by eight o'clock every evening. Which of the following things are you (not) supposed to do? Say your answers.

> ▷ *I am supposed to tell my parents the truth.*
> ▷ *I am not supposed to park my bicycle in the living-room.*

tell your parents the truth
park your bicycle in the living-room
help at home sometimes
tell your parents where you are going every time
   you go out
be punctual for meals
tell your parents if you will be home later than usual
eat everything that's on your plate
sit at the table in silence during meals
stay out all night without permission
take all your friends home to meet your parents
stay in bed until lunchtime at weekends
wear dirty shoes inside the house
play loud music late at night
go everywhere with your parents

b Work with a partner. Interview him/her about what he/she is supposed to do at home.

> ▷ YOU   *If you want to go out, are you always supposed to ask your parents?*
> PARTNER *I am supposed to ask them if I want to stay overnight at a friend's house.*

2 She had better . . .

What do you think they should do in the following situations? Say a sentence with **had better** and a sentence with **had better not** for each situation.

> ▷ Sylvia's exams are in two weeks' time.
> *She had better do some work.*
> *She had better not waste time.*

1 Sylvia's friends want to go to the cinema.
2 Sylvia wants to invite her friends to a party.
3 Sylvia's parents want to watch television, but Sylvia is playing very loud music in her room.
4 Sylvia's friend Anne wants Sylvia to go on holiday with her and her family.
5 Sylvia wants to go away for the weekend with some friends. Her parents are worried about her. They don't want her to go.
6 Sylvia has decided to try to explain to her parents why she isn't happy at home.

4 Class discussion

a Work with a partner. Choose the role of a parent or son/daughter. Imagine that you have a problem, for example about friends, clothes, spending money etc. Describe the problem from your point of view in a short paragraph. Look at the example, then think up your own.

> ▷ FATHER *My son is fourteen. He smokes and doesn't care about his health. He doesn't listen when I tell him it's bad for him.*
> SON   *I smoke because all the boys at school smoke. I don't really like it, but if you don't smoke you are an outsider. My father won't listen. He just criticizes.*

b Read both your points of view to the class. The class gives advice with **should/ought to**, **shouldn't**.

> ▷ *The father shouldn't criticize the son.*
> ▷ *The son ought to try to understand why his father criticizes him.*

33 Disco trouble may/might/could etc. + have

Grammar lesson

may/might/could etc. + have

We use **may/might/could have** + past participle to say what possibly happened in the past.
> *He **may/might have forgotten** about it.*
> *He **could have had** an accident on the way.*

We use **must have** + past participle to give an explanation for something that happened in the past.
> *Something **must have delayed** Jeff.*

The negative is **can't have**.
> *He **can't have forgotten** about Ann.*

We use **should/ought to have** + past participle to say what was a good thing to do in a past situation (but the person didn't do it).
> *Jeff **should have phoned** Ann.*

We use **needn't have** to say that something that happened in the past was not necessary.
> *They **needn't have been** so angry with each other.*

NICK   Jeff wanted to take Ann to the disco on Saturday. She waited for him at home for an hour, but he didn't turn up and he didn't phone. Ann was angry, so she phoned Jake Cook and asked him to take her to the disco. She knew that Jeff and Jake didn't like each other. Later that evening, Jeff saw Ann at the disco with Jake. Jeff felt angry, so he left immediately.

JANE   Something **must have delayed** Jeff. He **should have phoned** Ann to explain. He **could** even **have had** an accident on the way to her house.

NICK   He **might have forgotten** about the disco.

JANE   No. He **can't have forgotten** about Ann! But she **shouldn't have gone** out with Jake.

NICK   I agree. But they **needn't have been** so angry with each other.

---

turn up arrive

delay cause to be late

---

1 Reasons

a   Suggest possible reasons why Jeff didn't turn up at Ann's house. Use **might/may have** or **could have** + past participle. Write the reasons on the board. How many can you think of?

   ▷   *A visitor might have arrived unexpectedly.*
   ▷   *He could have lost his watch.*
   ▷   *He might have missed the bus.*

b   Take a class vote. The teacher reads out the reasons one by one. Put up your hand for the reason that you think is the most probable. You can vote only once. The teacher writes the number of votes on the board. Take turns to say the results.

   ▷   *Two pupils think that a visitor might have arrived unexpectedly.*
   ▷   *No one thinks that Jeff could have lost his watch.*

2 Explanations

Complete the sentences with **must have** or **can't have** + past participle.

▷ Later, Jeff said that he had phoned Ann before the disco.
Ann _can't have heard_ (hear) the phone.

1 Why didn't she hear the phone? The television _____ (be)
too loud.

2 Because Ann didn't answer the phone, Jeff _____ (think)
that she had already gone out.

3 After the disco, Ann didn't look very happy.
She _____ (enjoy) the evening.

4 Jake looked miserable too. He _____ (be) disappointed.

5 Jake didn't mention Jeff. Jake _____ (know) that Ann had
planned to go to the disco with him.

6 Jane didn't know the story about Ann and Jeff.
Ann _____ (tell) her.

7 A week after the evening at the disco, Ann got a letter from Jeff.
In the letter Jeff _____ (explain) what had happened and how
he had felt. Ann understood.

8 Next Saturday, Ann and Jeff are going to the cinema together.
They _____ (solve) their problems.

---

3 The right thing to do

a What do you think Jeff, Ann and Jake **should have**
done or **shouldn't have** done to avoid problems?
Write one sentence each about Jeff, Ann and Jake.
Write nine sentences altogether.

1 before the disco
   ▷ *I think Jeff should have been on time.*
   ▷ *Ann shouldn't have got angry.*
   ▷ *Jake shouldn't have taken Ann to the disco.*

2 at the disco

3 after the disco

b Discuss these questions for two minutes with a
partner. Then discuss your opinions with the class.
Give a reason for your opinion.

1 Should Ann have told Jake that she really
wanted to go to the disco with Jeff?

2 Should Ann have gone somewhere else
with Jake?

3 Should Jeff have been angry with Jake?

4 Sandra's story

a Read about Sandra and discuss the problem
with the class. Give opinions with
**might/may/could/must/should/shouldn't
have** etc.

When her parents went away for the weekend,
Sandra decided to invite her friends to a party.
Unfortunately, some glasses got broken. Sandra
didn't tell her parents about the party and she
lied about the glasses. Sandra's parents found
out the truth later and they punished her. They
didn't let her go out in the evenings for a month.

   ▷ *Sandra should have asked her parents about
   the party.*
   ▷ *Her parents might not have punished her
   if she had not lied.*

b Work with a partner. Think of another everyday
problem with friends, parents, brothers and
sisters etc. Write about the problem in the past
tense, as in (**a**). Tell the story to the class. The
class gives opinions with **could/might/must/
should have** etc.

34 Then and now   used to; would; be used to

Sharon, Jerry, Marion and Joe are talking about what they **used to be** like a few years ago. Can you guess who is speaking?

'I **used to be** very quiet. I'm an only child, so I'm **used to being** alone. I **would** spend hours in my room, reading and day-dreaming. I **didn't use to go** out much and I **never used to wear** fashionable clothes or make-up. Things have changed. Look at me now!'

'At fifteen I **used to be** a rebel and I always wore an old T-shirt and ripped jeans. I **would** go to pop concerts every week. I was crazy about music. I **used to** walk around all day carrying a radio. I was **used to being** told off at school because I didn't do enough work.'

'My friends and I **used to dress** all in black. At the time we thought it was great. We **would** go round the clothes stores, buying weird outfits and hats. My hair **used to be** green or pink – or both. We **were used to people staring** at us, but we **didn't use to care** about what others thought.'

Who doesn't say anything?

rebel	person who won't accept authority
ripped	torn
weird	very strange or unusual
outfit	clothes to wear together
stare	look long and hard at something

Grammar lesson

used to

We use **used to** + infinitive for things that happened regularly in the past or for things that were true in the past but are not true now. **used to** + infinitive expresses habits, actions and states in the past.

> *I **used to** be very quiet.*
> *We **didn't use to care** about what others thought.*
> *I **never used to** wear make-up.*
> *What **did** they **use to** be like?*

would

We use **would** + infinitive to talk about repeated actions in the past. It is not used with **be** or **have** when they express states in the past.

> *I **would** sit in my room for hours.*
> *I **would** go to pop concerts every week.*
> BUT *I **used to** have pink hair.*

be used to

We use **be used to** + **ing** form to say that something is familiar or usual.

> *I **am used to being** alone.*
> *We **were used to** people **staring** at us.*

1 How things used to be

a Make sentences with **used to**. Say the answers.

  ▷ Marion was very quiet.
     Marion used to be very quiet.

1 Marion spent hours in her room.
2 Sharon wore weird clothes.
3 Joe was crazy about pop music.
4 Marion didn't go out much.
5 Sharon dressed in black.
6 Joe wore ripped jeans.
7 Marion didn't wear fashionable clothes.
8 Joe was a rebel.
9 Sharon didn't care when people stared.
10 Sharon's hair was green and pink.

b Look at the pictures carefully. What else can you find that used to be different? Write down at least one thing about Sharon, Joe and Marion.

  ▷ *Joe used to have long hair.*

2 Life ten years ago

Can you use **would** instead of **used to**?
Write Yes or No.

  ▷ When Marion was fourteen she used to be
     very quiet. <u>*No*</u>

1 Joe always used to wear an old T-shirt.
     ———

2 Marion used to day-dream for hours. ———

3 Sharon used to have pink and green hair.
     ———

4 People used to stare at Sharon and her
     friends. ———

5 Joe and his friends used to carry radios
     everywhere they went. ———

6 Marion used to have long hair. ———

7 Marion used to sit in her room listening to
     music. ———

8 Sharon used to think that dressing in black
     looked great. ———

3 About Joe and Jerry

a This is what Jerry says about himself.
Use either the infinitive or the **ing** form of the verb in brackets.

'I used to <u>▷ *play*</u> (play) the drums
in my free time. We didn't use to

<u>1   </u> (do) much homework, so I

was used to <u>2   </u> (get) bad marks

in all subjects except music. We were used to

<u>3   </u> (play) in front of audiences

because we often used to

<u>4   </u> (play) at parties.

I was used to <u>5   </u> (stay) out late

and to <u>6   </u> (have) a good time.

That changed when I failed my school exams and

couldn't get a job.

b Look at the picture of Jerry and say how his appearance has changed.

  ▷ *He used to be much thinner.*

4 Have you changed?

Work with a partner. Take turns to ask and answer five questions about what you used to be like five years ago. Talk about looks, clothes, behaviour and what you used to like doing.

  ▷ PARTNER A *Did you use to have long hair?*
     PARTNER B *No, I didn't. Did you use to read comics?*
     PARTNER A *Yes, I did, but I don't now.*

I used to have a strange hairstyle, too.

NICK   It says in this magazine that loggerhead turtles are starting to die out. So many **have been killed**.

JANE   I didn't know that. Read it to me.

NICK   'Sneaky, Snappy, Solo and Penta, the stars of Care for the Wild's Greek Turtle Project, were some of the lucky ones. This is the story of how they **were helped**.

'On the Greek island of Cephalonia, hundreds of turtle nests **are made** on nesting beaches every summer. Unfortunately, female and baby turtles **are disturbed by** tourists. Only one in a thousand baby turtles survives.

'In 1988, a hundred turtle eggs **were taken** from their nest on Potomakia beach, Cephalonia, to England. The eggs **had been laid** too late in summer to develop. They **were incubated** at Southampton University and four baby turtles hatched. Four years later, when they weighed 25 kilos, the young turtles **were flown** back home.

'That was in May 1992. But the story doesn't end there. Blue tags **have been attached** to their back flippers, so they **will be recognized** easily.'

die out	no longer exist
survive	not die
incubate	keep an egg warm until it hatches
hatch	come out of an egg
tag	label
flipper	turtle's leg
attach	fix or fasten

Grammar lesson

The passive (1)

Simple tenses

We form these with a tense of **be** + past participle.

Present	*Nests **are made**.*
Past	*The babies **were helped**.*
Past perfect	*The eggs **had been laid**.*
Future	*The turtles **will be recognized**.*
Present perfect	*Many turtles **have been killed**.*
Future perfect	*They **will have been disturbed**.*

We can make a passive sentence from an active sentence:

Object

Active   *Somebody **flew** the* turtles *home.*

Passive   *The* turtles ***were flown** home.*

Subject

We use the passive if we do not know who does the action or if it is not important or not necessary to say who does it. The fact that the action happens is more important than the person who does it.

We can use **by + person/thing** if we wish to say who or what does the action.
   *Turtles are disturbed **by tourists**.*

1 Which is which?

Which verb forms are passive? Write the correct letters in the boxes.

	Yes	No	
they were flown	S	P	
they have hatched	O	N	
they will be helped	E	A	
they hadn't survived	L	A	
they are killed	K	N	
they have been seen	Y	A	

Now complete the sentence.

_____ is the name of a

_____ that _____

(rescue) by Care for the Wild.

2 The turtle story

Read the story again, then write the answers. Use passive verbs.

▷ Why are loggerhead turtles dying out?
Loggerhead turtles are dying out because so many have been killed.

1 What happened on Potomakia beach in 1988?

_____

_____

2 Why couldn't the turtle eggs develop?

_____

_____

3 What happened to the eggs at Southampton University?

_____

_____

4 What happened to the turtles in May 1992?

_____

_____

5 Why have tags been attached to the turtles?

_____

_____

A turtle laying eggs on the beach.

3 Turtle facts

a Put the verbs in the present simple passive.

Turtles ▷ *are found* _____ (find) in all the warm oceans of the world.

Turtles' nests ¹_____ (make) at night on sandy beaches. About one hundred eggs ²_____ (lay) in each nest. However, nesting turtles ³_____ (often disturb) by noise and lights from hotels and discos. When the babies leave the nest for the sea, they follow the light of the moon. But if they ⁴_____ (distract) by hotel lights, they run in the wrong direction. Babies who lose their way on the beach ⁵_____ (often kill) by birds. If they reach the sea, they ⁶_____ (sometimes injure) or even killed by speedboats.

b Work with a partner. One pupil is a TV journalist, the other is a turtle expert. Ask and answer questions in the present passive. To make your questions and answers, use the facts in (**a**) above.

> ▷ QUESTION   *How are baby turtles distracted when they run to the sea?*
>
>   ANSWER   *They are distracted by lights from hotels.*

---

distract confuse

injure hurt

4 A happy ending

Read the article about how Sneaky, Snappy, Solo and Penta were returned to their home.
Put the verbs in the past simple passive.

Care for the Wild's Turtle Project ▷ _was brought_ (bring)
to a happy end when the four turtles ¹_____ (fly)
back home to Cephalonia. Before they ²_____
(take) to the sea, the turtles ³_____ (weigh) and
their health ⁴_____ (check) by a vet. Then they
⁵_____ (place) in special wooden boxes and
⁶_____ (drive) to the coast, near Potomakia beach.
There they ⁷_____ (put) on board a Greek fishing
boat. The turtles ⁸_____ (accompany) by about
fifty people, including journalists, TV teams and schoolchildren.
Slowly, each turtle ⁹_____ (lower) into the clear,
warm water. As the turtles swam away, an underwater video film
¹⁰_____ (make).

Before their drive to the sea, the turtles were weighed.

> **vet** doctor for animals
>
> **accompany** go with someone
>
> **lower** put or let down

---

5 Informing the tourists

a Make sentences in the present perfect passive.
Say your answers.

> ▷ tourists – inform – about the nesting beaches
> *Tourists have been informed about the nesting beaches.*

1 talks and film shows/organize/in hotels
2 information brochures/print/for tourists and people on the islands
3 a speed limit/put/on motor boats
4 motor boats/ban/near nesting beaches
5 tourists/ask/not to leave litter on beaches
6 vehicles/prohibit/on nesting beaches
7 people/ask/not to use the beaches at night
8 warning signs/put up/on nesting beaches

> **ban** not allow
>
> **litter** rubbish
>
> **vehicle** car, lorry, bus etc.

b Work with a partner. Read (**a**) again, then close your books. Ask and answer four questions each, like this.

> ▷ YOU   *Have they put a speed limit on motor boats?*
>
> PARTNER   *Yes, a speed limit has been put on motor boats.*

6 Active to passive

Rewrite the sentences in the passive with **by**.

▷ At sea, speedboats injure turtles.

At sea, turtles are injured by speedboats.

1 Tourist activities have reduced the number of turtles.

_____

2 Tourists put sunbeds and sun umbrellas on nesting beaches.

_____

3 Noise and lights from discos frighten female turtles.

_____

4 Dogs dig up turtles' eggs.

_____

5 Large fish eat baby turtles.

_____

6 Scientists at Southampton University incubated four eggs.

_____

7 Care for the Wild had taken a hundred eggs from
Potomakia beach on Cephalonia.

_____

8 Care for the Wild returned the young turtles four years later.

_____

9 A vet checked the turtles' health.

_____

10 Greek and British television teams accompanied the turtles.

_____

11 Hundreds of tourists and Greek children watched the
fishing boat from the beach.

_____

12 A windsurfer saw Snappy two weeks later.

_____

7 Turtles in danger

Make the passive sentences active. Say your answers.

▷ Plastic bags are sometimes thrown into the sea by tourists.
Tourists sometimes throw plastic bags into the sea.

1 Plastic bags are sometimes eaten by turtles, because they look like jellyfish.
2 In some countries, turtles are caught by fishermen for food.
3 In some countries, dead turtles are sold to tourists by souvenir shop owners.
4 Live turtles are imported illegally by some rich countries.
5 Live turtles are sold by pet shop owners.
6 Turtles are poisoned by chemical waste in the sea.

jellyfish

illegal against the law

8 Class game

With a partner write passive sentences about turtles using the pictures. Make one sentence for each picture.

▷ *Turtles are killed by speedboats.*

❷

❸

❹

❺

❻

❶

Jenny and Nick are at the Seal Sanctuary in Cornwall.

JENNY   Look, Nick. The baby seal **is being fed** with a bottle.

KEEPER   Babies under three weeks old **have to be fed** with liquid fish.

NICK   What happened to this seal?

KEEPER   He **got thrown** against the rocks by a strong wave. Baby seals often **get injured** in stormy weather. He **may be kept** here for a few months.

JENNY   How many seals live around our coasts?

KEEPER   Two thirds of the world's Grey seals **are thought** to live around the British Coast. **It is estimated** that there are over a hundred thousand of them.

Then Nick and Jenny **were shown** the hospital. When they went in, a seal **was being examined** by a vet. The seal **was given** an injection, but he didn't like it, so unfortunately the assistant's finger **got bitten**.

Grammar lesson

The passive (2)

Continuous tenses

The passive is often used in the present continuous and in the past continuous.

Forms: **am/are/is** + **being** + past participle
was/were + **being** + past participle

The present continuous passive shows us that something is taking place now.
*Look. The baby seal **is being fed** with a bottle.*

The past continuous passive shows us that something was taking place at a particular time in the past.
*When Nick and Jenny went into the hospital, a seal **was being examined** by a vet.*

Infinitives

We form the passive infinitive with **be** + past participle. Verbs such as **can**, **will**, **must**, **may**, **might**, **have to**, **should** often come before it:
*Baby seals **have to be fed** with a bottle.*
*This seal **may be kept** here for a few months.*

The passive with **get**

In informal English **get** is used with some past participles instead of **be**, often with unfortunate actions that happen unexpectedly.
*Baby seals often **get injured**.*
*The assistant's finger **got bitten**.*

Also: **get lost, stolen, broken, caught, hurt killed, hit, stuck.**

keeper a person who looks after animals

liquid not in solid form, like something you drink

injection

Verbs with two objects

With verbs with two objects, for example **ask**, **give**, **offer**, **pay**, **tell**, **show**, **send** and **teach**, we can make a passive sentence in two ways.

> *An injection was given* to the seal.
> *The seal was given* an injection.

However, it is more usual to make a passive sentence which begins with a person (here: **the seal**).

Formal structures

In a formal style, verbs such as **believe**, **consider**, **estimate**, **think**, **say** and **know** have two passive forms.

Look at the structures with **that** and **to**.

> *It is estimated that* there are over a hundred thousand of them.
> *Two thirds of the world's Grey seals* **are thought to** live around the British coast.

1 The story of a rescue

Look at the pictures. Write what is being done to rescue the seal pup. Make the active sentences passive.

▷ Two helpers are examining an injured seal pup on the beach.

<u>An injured seal pup is being</u>
<u>examined by two helpers on the beach.</u>

1 They are putting the seal in a van.

_____

_____

2 They are driving him to the Seal Sanctuary.

_____

_____

3 They are carrying the pup into the hospital.

_____

_____

4 A vet is examining him.

_____

_____

5 A keeper is feeding him with a bottle.

_____

_____

2 Protest

All over the world, friends of animals are protesting. What is happening to the animals? Say answers in the present continuous passive, like this:

▷ Stop hunting whales!
  Whales are still being hunted.

1 Stop catching dolphins in nets!
2 Stop killing sharks!
3 Stop destroying turtles' nests!
4 Stop keeping dolphins in dolphinariums!
5 Stop training seals for circuses!
6 Stop shooting seals!

3 What was being done?

What was happening when Nick and Jenny arrived at the Seal Sanctuary? Rewrite the sentences in the past continuous passive.

▷ They were cleaning the pools.
  The pools were being cleaned.

1 A vet was examining a pup.

  _____

2 A keeper was preparing liquid fish food for the baby seals.

  _____

3 They were disinfecting the hospital.

  _____

4 They were feeding the larger seals.

  _____

5 A vet was treating an injured pup.

  _____

6 A guide was showing visitors round.

  _____

---

disinfect clean thoroughly to kill germs

4 What has to be done?

a Work in two teams. You get one point for each correct sentence. Make the active sentences passive. Use a passive infinitive and say your answers, like this:

▷ We have to clean the pools every two days.
  The pools have to be cleaned every two days.

1 We must fill the pools with fresh sea water.
2 We have to feed the pups four times a day.
3 We must disinfect the hospital once a day.
4 We could help more animals if we had more room.
5 We are going to build two more pools this year.
6 The rough sea may wash a baby miles away from its mother.
7 We may keep an injured seal here for several months.
8 We must teach young seals to feed themselves.

5 They are given help

Rewrite the sentences. Begin with the word in italics, like this:

▷ Help is given to *sick seals* at the Sanctuary.
  Sick seals are given help at the Sanctuary.

1 Liquid fish is given to *baby seals*.
2 The hospital is shown to *visitors*.
3 They inform *visitors* about the work at the Sanctuary.
4 The keeper told *Jenny* never to touch a baby seal.
5 They gave *Nick and Jenny* some information brochures.
6 The keepers tell *you* lots of facts about seals.

dolphins

killer whale

6 It is known . . .

Write the sentences in another way, like this:

▷ We know that dolphins are highly intelligent.

It _is known that dolphins are highly intelligent._

Dolphins _are known to be highly intelligent._

1 We believe that some kinds of sea animals are dying out.

It _____

Some kinds of sea animals _____

penguin

2 We do not know why so many dolphins die in British waters.

It _____

3 The monk seal is one of the world's largest seals.
We know that it weighs around 300 kilos.

The monk seal _____

4 We think that the monk seal is Europe's most threatened species.

It _____

5 We estimate that the monk seal travels up to 200 kilometres a day to find food.

The monk seal _____

7 Class discussion

With your teacher, talk about sea animals which are in danger, for example dolphins and whales. Discuss these questions. Give reasons for your opinions.

Should dolphins be kept in dolphinariums?

Should sea animals be trained to do tricks?

Should whaling be allowed?

Write the results of the discussion in a short paragraph.

sea lion

humpback whale

shark

NICK   You're fond **of** animals, aren't you, Ben?

BEN   Yes, I'm particularly interested **in** rare animals. Look **at** this picture **of** the aye-aye.

NICK   It looks **like** something **from** outer space. What's the purpose **of** such long thin fingers? They look **like** twigs.

BEN   Well, the aye-aye is a rainforest animal. It eats insects which live **under** the bark **of** trees. It's got very good ears. It's capable **of** hearing the slightest sound. It puts its ear **next to** the bark **of** a tree and listens **for** signs **of** movement. Then it quickly bites a hole **in** the bark and puts its middle finger **into** the hole to pull out the insect. It also uses its middle finger **for** combing its hair.

NICK   What else do you know **about** aye-ayes?

BEN   They live only **in** Madagascar. They sleep **during** the day and are active **at** night. They often hang upside-down **from** branches. And the strong claws **on** their feet are used **as** hooks.

NICK   I'm surprised **at** how much you know. Why are they called aye-ayes?

BEN   **Because of** the strange noises they make. They cry 'aye! aye!' **by** blowing **through** their noses. The island people are frightened **of** the noises they make.

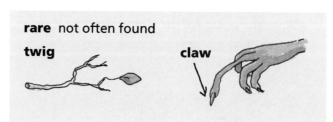

rare not often found

twig   **claw**

Grammar lesson

Prepositions

We use prepositions (**in, under, for**) mostly before nouns or pronouns. Remember that English prepositions are not always used in the same way as prepositions in your language.

Place

in, on, at, next to, near, in front of, behind, under, above, on top of, below, between, inside, outside, opposite tell us *where* things are or *where* things happen.

We usually use **in** for something which is inside an area, building or object.
> **in** *the rainforests,* **in** *South America,* **in** *the bark*

We usually use **on** for a position on a line or surface.
> **on** *its feet,* **on** *the coast*

We usually use **at** to describe a place at a point.
> **at** *the top of the tree*

Here are some common expressions:

on the right/left	**in the picture**
on the page	**in the middle**
at the back/front	**in the background**
at the top/bottom	

Movement

up, down, into, over, through, across, along, past, out of, from, onto, towards, from . . . to tell us about *movement* or *direction*.
> *The aye-aye puts its finger* **into** *the hole.*
> *It travels* **through** *the forest* **from** *tree* **to** *tree.*

Time

in, on, at, during, after, before, until/till tell us *when* something happens.
> *The aye-aye sleeps* **during** *the day and is active* **at** *night.*

Prepositions + ing

We use **for** + **ing** to show *purpose.*
> *It uses its middle finger* **for** *com**bing** its hair.*

We use **by** + **ing** to say *how* we do something.
> *The aye-aye make strange noises* **by** *blo**wing** through its nose.*

as and like

We use **as** to talk about the *function* or *role* of something, especially after the verbs **use, dress** and **work.**
> *The claws on the aye-aye's feet are used* **as** *hooks.*

We use **like** to express that something is similar to something else.
> *The aye-aye jumps from tree to tree,* **like** *a monkey.*

We use **like** after the verb **look.**
> *Its middle finger looks* **like** *a twig.*

Prepositions after nouns, adjectives and verbs

We often use a particular preposition after an adjective, noun or verb. We have to learn these by heart. Here are some examples.

Adjectives	*Nouns*
afraid **of**	attitude **to/towards**
bored **with/by**	cause **of**
capable **of**	damage **to**
fond **of**	example **of**
full **of**	knowledge **of**
interested **in**	purpose **of**
similar **to**	reason **for**
surprised **at**	solution **to**
tired **of**	success **in**
worried **about**	trouble **with**

Verbs
agree **with** somebody/something
approve **of** somebody/something
believe **in** somebody/something
belong **to** somebody/something
insist **on** something
succeed **in** something
suffer **from** something

Many people do not **approve of** *destroying the rainforests.*
Rainforests have **suffered from** *felling and burning.*

1 Quick quiz

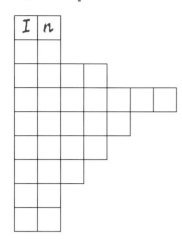

Write the missing prepositions in the puzzle.
Write all the words *across*.

▷ Ben is very interested *in*_____ animals.

1 Rainforests are full _____ unusual animals and plants.

2 The rainforests suffer _____ man's mistakes.

3 We must change people's attitudes _____ rainforests.

4 People ought to be worried _____ the destruction that is going on there.

5 I agree _____ you.

6 What are the reasons _____ the destruction?

7 Scientists have very little knowledge _____ rainforest plants.

8 The rainforests belong _____ us all.

2 Aye-aye facts

a Complete the facts about aye-ayes using suitable prepositions. Sometimes more than one answer is possible.

▷ The aye-aye lives only *in*_____ Madagascar.

1 Its home is _____ the rainforests _____ the east coast of the island.

2 It sleeps _____ the day and is active _____ night.

3 It uses the strong claws _____ its feet _____ hooks.

4 It uses its hands _____ feeding or cleaning.

5 The aye-aye sometimes eats coconuts. It dips its middle finger _____ the coconut milk.

6 Its long middle fingers look _____ twigs.

7 The aye-aye also uses its middle fingers _____ scratching.

8 Aye-ayes jump _____ tree _____ tree, _____ monkeys.

9 The people of Madagascar are afraid _____ the strange noise that the aye-aye makes.

10 It cries 'aye! aye!' _____ blowing _____ its nose.

b Work with a partner. Ask and answer five questions about aye-ayes. Use prepositions in your answers.

▷ YOU   *Where do aye-ayes live?*
  PARTNER *They live in the rainforests on the coast of Madagascar.*

destruction great damage, ruin

3 The Amazon rainforest

a Write in the missing prepositions. Choose from **along**, **for**, **from**, **in**, **of**, **on**, **through**, **to**, **until**, **within**. If you think that two answers are possible, write both.

▷ *Until* _____ a hundred years ago, countries

▷ *on* _____ the equator were covered with

rainforests. More than half of all the types of

plants and animals [1]_____ earth lived

there.

The largest rainforest is Amazonia [2]_____

South America. It covers an area [3]_____

about 6.5 million square kilometres. It takes its

name from the River Amazon which flows

[4]_____ the northern part of Brazil.

Thousands [5]_____ different kinds of

animals, birds and butterflies live there. But the

rainforest has suffered [6]_____ felling and

burning. Now long dusty roads lead

[7]_____ the forest. What are the reasons

[8]_____ the destruction? Trees are burnt

or cut down [9]_____ their hardwood. The

land is used [10]_____ farms, mines and

cattle ranches.

There has already been a lot of damage

[11]_____ the plants and animals of the

rainforest. If the destruction is not stopped,

[12]_____ thirty years all the trees will

be gone.

b Work with a partner. One partner is an expert on tropical rainforests. The other is a journalist who is interviewing the expert. Take turns to be the journalist and the expert. Ask and answer five questions each about rainforests, using prepositions.

▷ JOURNALIST *Where are rainforests found?*
EXPERT *Along the Equator. In South America, in Africa, in parts of Asia.*

4 Find the animals

Look at the picture very carefully. There are some animals, insects and birds hiding. Can you find them? When you have found one, describe where it is to the class. The class must guess which animal etc. you are describing.

First, say where they are on the picture, using **at the top/bottom**, **on the left/right**, **in the middle/background** etc.

▷ *I have found an insect on the right, at the bottom of the picture. It is hiding behind a large leaf . . .*

38 If I win, you lose

Conditional sentences types 1 and 2; **unless**; **as long as, provided that** etc.

JENNY   It's raining. **If** it **doesn't** stop, we'll play Truth or Tact.

NICK   That's a good idea. We'll play **when** Tom **comes**.

BEN   How do you play?

NICK   There are questions on the cards. You have to say what you **would** do **if** a certain thing **happened**. There are some answers on the back of the card. **If you choose** the best solution, you **get** the most points. You have to decide whether it is better to be truthful or tactful. For example, **if you saw** a friend breaking a neighbour's window by mistake, **would** you **tell** the neighbour or **would** you keep quiet?

BEN   That's a difficult question. I'm not sure what **I'd** do.

JENNY   In some questions you don't get any points **unless** you tell the truth.

BEN   All right, I'll play **as long as** I can keep the scores.

NICK   No, Ben. If you **kept** the scores, you **might** cheat. We'll ask Tom to do that.

> **tact** not telling the whole truth, in order not to hurt someone's feelings
>
> **score** the number of points you win in a game

Grammar lesson

Conditional sentences

We usually make conditional sentences with **if**. When we put the **if** part of the sentence first, we usually put a comma (,) after it.

Type 1

For facts that do not change or things that always happen (for example, in the rules of a game), we use the present simple in the **if** clause and in the main clause.

> *If you **choose** the best solution, you **get** the most points.*

We use **if** + present simple and **will/won't** in the main clause for things that will possibly happen.

> *If it **doesn't stop** raining, we'll stay at home.*

Type 2

We use **if** + past and **would** ('d) in the main clause for situations that are 'unreal'.
We imagine a result in the present or future.

> *If you **saw** it, what **would** you do?*

Instead of **would** we can use **might** (= would possibly) or **could** (= would be able to) in the main clause.

> *If you **kept** the scores, you **might** cheat.*

unless

We can use **unless** in a conditional sentence. It means 'if . . . not'.

> *You don't get any points **unless** you tell the truth.*
> (= if you do not tell the truth)

as long as, provided/providing that

All mean 'on condition that . . . , only if . . .'
They are more emphatic than **if**.

> *I'll play **as long as/ provided that/ providing that** I can keep the scores.*

if and when

Use **if** for something that is only possible, not certain. Use **when** for something that is certain.
We'll play if Tom comes.
We'll play when Tom comes.

in case

in case means 'because it is possible that . . .'
*We'll ask Tom to keep the scores **in case** Ben tries to cheat.*

1 If it rains

Complete the sentences with the present simple or **will**/**won't** + infinitive.

1 If it doesn't rain, we ___*will stay*___ (go) swimming.

2 We _____ (play) Truth or Tact if we can't go out.

3 If you don't know how to play, Nick _____ (explain) the rules to you.

4 If you are not sure what to say, you just _____ (have) to guess.

5 You _____ (not get) any points if you make the wrong choice.

6 Tom _____ (miss) the game if he doesn't come soon.

7 When you score a point, you _____ (write) the number down.

8 If you get the highest score, you _____ (win) the game.

9 If Ben cheats, we _____ (not let) him play again.

10 If it rains tomorrow, we _____ (play) the game again.

2 Choices

Complete the sentences. Choose **a**, **b** or **c**.
Say your answers.

▷ ___*b*___ we go to the football match, we can play again on Saturday.

   a when
   b unless
   c in case

1 I'll play the game _____ I can keep the scores.

   a in case
   b as long as
   c unless

2 We'll play Truth or Tact _____ you don't cheat.

   a in case
   b provided that
   c when

3 I'll explain the rules to you _____ you don't know them.

   a when
   b unless
   c if

4 Nick won't play the game _____ everyone plays.

   a unless
   b providing that
   c when

5 You score a point _____ you answer the question correctly.

   a as long as
   b in case
   c unless

6 You ought to ring Tom _____ he forgets to come this afternoon.

   a provided that
   b as long as
   c in case

7 _____ it doesn't stop raining, we'll stay at home.

   a as long as
   b when
   c if

8 We'll start playing again _____ Tom arrives.

   a when
   b in case
   c unless

3 Truth or Tact?

a Work with a partner. Read the difficult situations below and take turns to say what you would do in each situation. For each situation say which solution you would choose and why. Then say what might or could happen if you chose the other two solutions.

▷ *I would choose **a** because he wouldn't know that it was untrue. If I chose **b**, he might find out that I had lied. If I chose **c**, I might hurt his feelings.*

b Stay with your partner. Write five more difficult situations like the ones in (**a**). Read them to the class and discuss the possible solutions.

1

You have invited ten friends to a party. At school you see a boy you didn't invite to the party because you don't like him very much. He knows about the party and he wants to know why you didn't invite him. Would you:

a tell him that you were only allowed to invite ten people?

b tell him that his invitation must have got lost in the post?

c tell him that you didn't like him?

2

You are late for school and you have left your bus pass at home. You don't want to have to spend more money on a bus ticket. Would you:

a go home and get your bus pass?

b buy a bus ticket?

c hide under one of the bus seats and hope the conductor didn't see you?

3

A good friend has borrowed money from you several times but hasn't paid it back. He/she has just asked you again to lend him/her £5. Would you:

a lend him/her the money and say nothing?

b refuse to lend the money and tell him/her why?

c say that you didn't have any money?

4

You have spent a lot of time doing a Geography project for school. Someone in your class wants to copy your project instead of doing one him/herself. Would you:

a tell him/her that you got a very low mark for your work?

b let him/her copy it and say nothing?

c refuse and tell your teacher?

5

Your best friend has written a song. He/she thinks it is wonderful. You think it is terrible. He/she asks you for your opinion. Would you:

a say that it was the best song you'd ever heard?

b say that you thought it was quite good but that he/she should ask for other people's opinions as well?

c say that it was the worst thing you'd ever heard?

6

Your aunt has knitted a jumper for your birthday. It doesn't fit you and you don't like it. She spent a long time knitting it for you. Would you:

a thank her and wear it every time you saw her?

b tell her it didn't fit and ask her to knit you another one?

c thank her and give it to someone you didn't like?

4 If . . .

a Look at the questions below and write a suitable answer.
Then take turns to read your answers to the class.

▷ If it rained on your birthday, what would you do?

*If it rained on my birthday, I'd go
to the cinema with my friends.*

1   If someone gave you £100, what would you buy?

_____

_____

2   If you found a dog with a broken leg, what would
you do?

_____

_____

3   If you won a plane ticket for anywhere in the
world, where would you go?

_____

_____

4   If you forgot your best friend's birthday, what
would you say?

_____

_____

5   If you saw someone robbing a bank, what
would you do?

_____

_____

6   If you lost your homework, what would you do?

_____

_____

7   If you found someone's wallet in the street,
what would you do with it?

_____

_____

8   If you lost your house key, what would you do?

_____

_____

9   If you met a famous pop star, what would you
say to him/her?

_____

_____

10   If you could be a film star, who would you be?

_____

_____

b Work with a partner. Write five more questions
with **if** + past simple and **would**. Read and answer
your questions round the class.

5   A million dollars

Have you got a good memory? Make two teams.
Each pupil in Team A says what he/she would do
if he/she had a million dollars. It can be serious
or funny. Pupils in Team B must try to remember
what each pupil in Team A said. Score one point
for each correctly remembered sentence. Then
play the game again with Team B's sentences.

▷   *If X had a million dollars, he would buy a yacht.*
If Y had a million dollars, she would go to Hollywood.

39 Silly old crow   Conditional sentences type 3; **I wish**; **if**

The fox and the crow

A crow was sitting at the top of a tall tree, holding a large piece of meat in his beak. Underneath the tree was a big, hungry fox. When he saw the meat he thought, ' **I wish I had** that meat. **If only I could** make that silly old crow drop it, **I could** have it for supper.' So he said, 'Mr Crow, you are the most beautiful bird I have ever seen. **If only I were** as beautiful as you! I am sure that you sing beautifully too.'

The crow was very pleased to hear this and opened his beak to show how well he could sing. Of course, he dropped the meat. The fox quickly ran and picked it up. The crow was furious. He shouted at the fox: '**If you hadn't spoken** to me, **I wouldn't have dropped** the meat. Give it back to me at once!' The fox just laughed and ran off with the meat. That evening, the fox was happy and he had a full stomach. He smiled and thought, 'Silly old crow, **if only** he **had been born** with a brain, he **could have eaten** the meat himself!'

The rat and the lion

A rat was walking through the forest one day when he trod on a lion's paw. '**I wish I hadn't done** that,' he thought, 'the lion will probably eat me now.' Fortunately the lion was in a good mood, so he let the rat go free. The rat thanked the lion and promised to repay his kindness.

A few weeks later, while he was out hunting, the lion accidentally got caught in a net. '**If I hadn't been** so careless, **I wouldn't have fallen** into this trap. **If only I could escape** from it,' he thought. He struggled for a long time but he could not break the net. He roared as loudly as he could and all the animals of the forest ran to help him. They each tried to rescue the lion, but none of them was able to. '**I wish we could** help you,' said the wolf, 'but we are not strong enough.' The rat was determined to help his friend. He started chewing through the net. Two hours later, the lion was free. The lion was very grateful. '**If you hadn't trodden** on my paw last week, **we wouldn't have met**,' he said, 'and **I might have died**.'

Grammar lesson

Conditional sentences type 3

We use **if** + past perfect + **would have** + past participle for *unreal* situations in the past.

If clause   *Main clause*
past perfect   **would have** + past participle

We imagine a condition or situation in the past which is impossible.

> *If the fox **hadn't spoken** to the crow, the crow **wouldn't have dropped** the meat.* (but the fox spoke to him)

Instead of **would have**, we can use **might have** or **could have** in the main clause.

> *If the crow **had been born** with more brains, he **could have eaten** the meat himself.*

I wish

We use **wish** + past simple to talk about something in the present that we regret.

> *I **wish I had** that meat.*

We use **wish** + past perfect to talk about something in the past that we regret. We cannot change what did or didn't happen.

> *I **wish I hadn't dropped** the meat.*

Note also **I wish I could** (do something) to talk about something in the present or the future.

> *I **wish I could** make the crow drop the meat.*

if only

We can use **if only** instead of **I wish** with the same use of tenses.

> *If only I **was/were** as beautiful as you.*
> *If only I **hadn't dropped** the meat.*
> *If only I **could** make him drop it.*

1 If the crow hadn't . . .

Complete the sentences with the past perfect of the words in brackets, or with **would/wouldn't have** + past participle.

▷   If the crow hadn't been in the tree, the fox
<u>wouldn't have seen</u> (not see) him.

1   If the fox _____
(not be) hungry, he wouldn't have wanted the crow's meat.

2   If the fox hadn't been so clever, he
_____ (not trick)
the crow.

3   If the crow hadn't been so silly, he
_____ (not listen)
to the fox.

4   If the crow _____
(not open) his beak, he wouldn't have dropped the meat.

5   If the fox hadn't had a full stomach, he
_____ (not be) happy.

6   If the lion had been in a bad mood, he
_____ (eat) the rat.

7   If the rat hadn't been grateful, he
_____ (not promise) to
repay the lion's kindness.

8   If the lion _____
(not be) careless, he wouldn't have fallen into the net.

9   If the animals _____
(not hear) the lion's roar, they wouldn't have gone to help him.

10   If the rat hadn't wanted to help the lion, he
_____ (not chew)
through the net.

2 Life in the 1790s

Imagine how different life would have been, if you had lived two hundred years ago.

a Write ten sentences. Say what you **would/wouldn't have done** or **had**, like this:

▷ *If I had lived two hundred years ago, I would have worn different clothes.*

▷ *If I had lived two hundred years ago, I wouldn't have had a bicycle.*

b Write ten more sentences. Say what you **could/couldn't have done** or **had**, like this:

▷ *If I had lived two hundred years ago, I could have gone to school in a carriage.*

▷ *If I had lived two hundred years ago, I couldn't have spoken to my friends on the telephone.*

---

3 Panic at the bank

It was a quiet morning at the bank in Little Rissington. The cashiers were counting money, there were two customers in the bank and the manager was having a cup of coffee.

Suddenly a robber ran in. He was carrying a gun. One of the customers, an old lady, screamed and tried to run out of the bank. She slipped and fell over. The other customer tried to pull the robber to the floor. A cashier rang the alarm bell. The manager telephoned the police. The robber panicked and jumped out of a window. A policeman arrived. First he helped the old lady and then he chased the robber. The robber escaped.

a Work with a partner. Look carefully at the story. Make as many true sentences as you can. Use **if** + past perfect + **might/might not have** + past participle, like this:

▷ *If the manager hadn't been drinking coffee, he might have noticed the robber coming into the bank.*

b What **would/wouldn't** you have done if you had been the following people? Take turns to say two sentences each.

If you had been the manager, . . .
If you had been the cashier, . . .
If you had been the old lady, . . .
If you had been the second customer, . . .
If you had been the policeman, . . .
If you had been the robber, . . .

4 Regrets

a Look at the people in the pictures below. They all regret something they have done. What do you think they are saying? Write two sentences for each picture. Use **if only/I wish** + past simple or past perfect.

▷ *I wish I hadn't dyed my hair green.*

b Now say sentences with **I wish I could . . .**
What do the people in the pictures wish they could do?

▷ *I wish I could make my hair grow faster.*

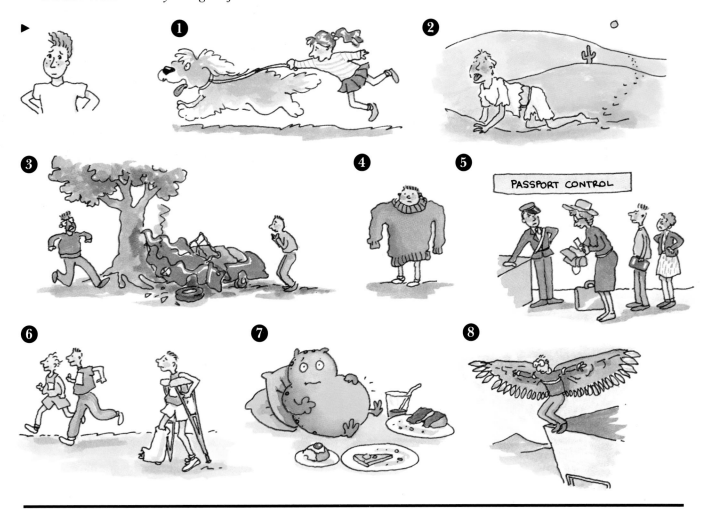

5 If only . . .

a Think about the things you would like to have or the kind of person you would like to be. Make a list of ten sentences using **if only** + past simple + **I could**, like this:

▷ *If only I had more pocket money, I could buy some new clothes.*
▷ *If only I were a famous actor, I could live in a house with a big swimming pool.*

b Think about all the things you wanted to do last year but didn't do. Make a list of ten sentences with **I wish** + past perfect, like this:

▷ *I wish I had passed my history exam.*
▷ *I wish I hadn't forgotten my friend's birthday.*

c Take turns to read your sentences round the class.

Which is your star sign?

AQUARIUS January 21 – February 19

You **enjoy being** independent and **like saying** what you think. You have **difficulty in accepting** other people's opinions. You **like belonging** to clubs and **talking** to people. You have original ideas and are **good at inventing**.

PISCES February 20 – March 20

You **love dancing** and you are **fond of writing** poetry and **making** music. You are not very **good at organizing**. You **dislike planning**. You **enjoy helping** people, but you try to **avoid taking** responsibility.

ARIES March 21 – April 20

You **hate following** a routine. You **enjoy playing** energetic sports and you **like taking** part in races. You **don't mind taking** risks. You don't **worry about hurting** the feelings of others.

TAURUS April 21 – May 21

You **prefer doing** quiet things, like **painting** and **listening** to music. You **avoid doing** things that are energetic. You **don't mind accepting** routines and rules.

GEMINI May 22 – June 21

You are **quick at picking up** new ideas and are **better at doing** mental work than manual work. You are easily **bored with doing** the same things. You **enjoy discussing** things with people.

CANCER June 22 – July 23

You **like looking after** and **protecting** people. **Collecting** is often a hobby. You **love swimming** and all water sports.

LEO July 24 – August 23

You usually **succeed in getting** what you want. You are **fond of playing** games and you **enjoy taking** risks. You are **good at organizing**. You often **insist on doing** what you want. You **love acting**.

VIRGO August 24 – September 23

You are not **keen on taking** the lead. But you always do things that **need doing**. **Making** things is a favourite activity. You **like paying** attention to detail.

LIBRA September 24 – October 23

You are **good at being** diplomatic. You **hate quarrelling**. You **prefer** quiet activities, such as **sunbathing**, **painting**, **writing** and **reading**.

SCORPIO October 24 – November 22

You sometimes have **difficulty in controlling** your temper. You are a good detective. You **love finding out** answers and **solving** puzzles. You **like** active sports such as **boxing**, karate and water sports.

SAGITTARIUS November 23 – December 21

Being free is important to you. You **hate being** forced into a routine. You are **capable of putting** a lot of enthusiasm into your interests. You **like walking**, **riding** and **doing** outdoor sports.

CAPRICORN December 22 – January 20

You are **capable of working** very hard. You **dislike** people **being** untidy. You **can't stand wasting** time on unnecessary things. You **like organizing** and you **don't mind being** alone. You **enjoy reading.**

---

independent free to do things yourself and make your own decisions

mental with your brain

manual with your hands

Grammar lesson

Gerunds

We can use the **ing** form as a noun. We call it a gerund. It can be subject or object.

Subject   *Painting is one of your hobbies.*
Object   *You enjoy painting.*

We use a gerund after the following verbs.

avoid	don't mind	postpone
can't bear	enjoy	practise
can't help	give up	put off
can't stand	keep on	risk
dislike	miss	suggest

*You **don't mind being** alone.*

We use a gerund or an infinitive after the following verbs.

continue	like	prefer
hate	love	start
intend	need	

*You **like taking** part in races.*
*You **like to take** part in races.*

We use a gerund after a preposition. The list shows verbs, adjectives and nouns which are followed by a preposition + gerund.

apologize for
approve of
believe in
insist on
succeed in
worry about

bored with
capable of
fond of
good at
interested in
keen on
pleased about
tired of

difficulty in
reason for
way of

    doing something

*You have **difficulty in accepting** the opinions of others.*
*You **insist on doing** what you want.*
*You soon get **tired of doing** the same thing.*

We use a gerund when a verb follows **need** or **want**. It has a passive meaning.

*. . . things that **need doing***
(things that should be done)

1 Hobbies

a Write a list of your hobbies and activities. Take turns to tell the class.

> ▷ *My hobbies are reading, listening to music and painting.*

b Write a list of five things that you love doing and five things that you hate doing. Read your list to the class.

> ▷ *I love getting presents.*
> *I hate waiting in queues.*

c Look for your star sign and read the description again. What does it say about your hobbies or interests? Is it true for you? Tell the class.

> ▷ *My star sign is Sagittarius. It says that I like things such as walking, riding and doing outdoor sports. It is true, although I can't ride. I also like playing basketball.*

I like doing outdoor sports, too.

2 In my class

a. Complete the second half of the sentence with the verb in the **ing** form.

b. Add the name of a person in your class for whom you think this might be true. It doesn't have to be very serious!

▷ _David_ _____ enjoys **wasting** _____ (waste) time.

1 _____ hates _____ (watch) football matches.

2 _____ is interested in _____ (learn) languages.

3 _____ likes _____ (sit) in the sun and _____ (listen) to pop music.

4 _____ soon gets tired of _____ (do) the same things.

5 _____ is good at _____ (organize) parties.

6 _____ loves _____ (argue) and _____ (discuss) things.

7 _____ is fond of _____ (collect) things.

8 _____ doesn't approve of _____ (smoke).

9 _____ has difficulty in _____ (get) to school on time.

10 _____ dislikes _____ (save) money.

11 _____ can't stand _____ (watch) romantic films.

12 _____ is thinking of _____ (become) a rock star.

---

3 Guess the sign

a Choose one of the star signs on page 130 (but not your own) and remember the details. Do not tell anyone which one you have chosen. The class must guess the star sign by asking questions. In your answers you must use the information you have learnt or remembered.

▷ *Do you like making things?*
Yes, I do. OR *No, I don't.*

b Try to guess your teacher's star sign by asking questions from the descriptions.

▷ CLASS   *Are you good at organizing?*
TEACHER   *My star sign says 'No'.*
CLASS   *Do you enjoy arguing?*
TEACHER   *My star sign says 'Yes'.*

4 What needs doing?

Do you always do things that need doing?

Say three things that need doing . . .

▷ in your room
My desk needs tidying.

1 at home
2 in your classroom
3 in your school
4 in your town
5 in your country

5 Work it out

a Work in pairs. Read what Colin, Sarah and Brian say about themselves. Try to work out what their star signs are by comparing the descriptions on page 130. Tell the class the reasons for your answers. If other pupils have a different opinion, discuss why.

> PAIR A   *We think Brian is Leo because he . . .*
> PAIR B   *We don't agree. We think that Brian is Capricorn because . . .*

COLIN

I enjoy doing lazy things, because I'm not a very active person. I'm not ambitious. I have a lot of friends and I love spending time with them. I never quarrel and I like helping others to solve their difficulties.

SARAH

I'm a busy, active person. I prefer moving around to staying in one place. I enjoying using my brain, but I sometimes have difficulty in concentrating. I love discussing, but sometimes I'm too talkative. I'm interested in doing lots of things, all at the same time.

BRIAN

I can't stand doing the same thing over and over again. I'm adventurous and competitive. I have a lot of energy and I like taking risks. Sometimes I'm a bit selfish. If I want something, I keep on trying until I succeed in getting it.

b Which of the three young people would you choose to be your friend? Why? Write the reasons for your choice in a short paragraph.

> *I would choose Brian to be my friend because he doesn't like doing boring things.*

6 Is it true?

a Work in groups. Sit with pupils who have the same star sign as you.

In the group, read through the character description again and discuss what is generally true for you. Be honest! One member of the group tells the class what you agree with and what you disagree with.

> *Our star sign is Cancer. It says we like looking after and protecting people. This is true because we all like looking after small children and animals.*
> *It says collecting is often a hobby, but only two of us collect things.*

b Summarize what your group thinks in a short paragraph.

41 Computer crazy   make and let; to + infinitive

When Alan was ten, he **seemed to be** very interested in computers. His mother knew that he **would love to have** one, but she couldn't **afford to buy** him one. He learned **how to use** a friend's computer, but he **couldn't wait to get** one of his own.

His mother **decided to give** him a computer for his twelfth birthday. At first she only **let him use** it for an hour a day. She didn't **want it to damage** his eyes.

By the time Alan was fifteen he had become very good at using his computer, but it was his only hobby. His mother **wanted him to go** out and do things, but he had very few friends. Nobody could **persuade him to do** anything and nothing could **make him turn** his computer off.

In the end, his mother **threatened to turn** off the electricity. Alan went to bed and **pretended to be** asleep, but at midnight he got up **to work** at the computer again. He didn't **want to sleep** or **to eat**. He just couldn't **bear to be** away from his computer.

Alan's mother didn't know **what to do**. Her sixteen-year-old son had become a computer addict. Not even the family doctor knew **how to help**. One morning Alan's mother found him lying on the bedroom floor. He had collapsed with exhaustion. Two weeks in hospital finally **made Alan realize** that his computer had become a dangerous obsession.

Now Alan is eighteen. He has lots of friends and hobbies. He **hopes to study** computer science at university and **would like to find** a job in computer research.

---

damage hurt

collapse fall down because you are weak or tired

exhaustion the state of being extremely tired

obsession something that you think about so much that it controls your life

Grammar lesson

make and let

After **make** and **let** we use an object + infinitive without **to**.

> *Alan's mother **let him use** the computer for an hour a day.*
> *She tried to **make him turn** it off.*

to + infinitive

After verbs

We use **to** + infinitive after the following verbs.

afford	expect	offer	refuse
agree	hope	plan	seem
arrange	learn	pretend	threaten
can't wait	manage	promise	want
decide			

> *She couldn't **afford to buy** him a computer.*
> *He **pretended to be** asleep.*
> *He didn't **want to sleep** or **to eat**.*

We also use **to** + infinitive after **would** + **like/love/prefer/hate**.

> *She knew that he **would like to have** a computer.*

But if there is no **would**, an **ing** form often follows.

> *He loved using the computer.*

We can use an object + **to** + infinitive after the following.

advise	help	persuade	tell
allow	invite	prefer	want
ask	order	teach	warn
expect			

> *She couldn't **persuade him to stop**.*
> *His friends **wanted him to go** out with them.*

After question words

We use **to** + infinitive after the question words **when**, **what**, **where**, **how** (but not after **why**).

> *She didn't know **what to do**.*
> *The doctor didn't know **how to help** him.*

For purpose

We use (**in order**) **to** + infinitive to show purpose or the reason why someone does something.

> *At midnight Alan got up **to work** again.*

1 What did she let him do?

a Complete the sentences about Alan with the correct form of **make** or **let**.

▷ Before Alan had a computer, his friend ___Let___ him use his.

1 When Alan was twelve, his mother _____ him use the computer for an hour a day.

2 Then she _____ him turn it off.

3 She said Alan shouldn't _____ the computer damage his eyes.

4 At first, Alan _____ his friends play games on his computer.

5 Alan's friends tried to _____ him go out with them, but he didn't want to.

6 His mother tried to _____ him take up other hobbies, but she couldn't persuade him.

7 The family doctor couldn't _____ him change his attitude either.

8 A stay in hospital finally _____ him realize that his computer was ruining his life.

9 If he hadn't stopped when he did, Alan might have _____ himself extremely ill.

10 Alan _____ his obsession take over his life.

b When you were ten, what did your parents let you do? What did they make you do? Write a short paragraph.

2 Helping a friend

Work with a partner. Imagine that you have five friends who have problems, like Alan. With your partner, invent some problems and say how you tried to help. Write five sentences using the verbs below + **him/her** + **to** + infinitive. Describe the problem first, like this:

▷ *We have a friend who wants to stop smoking, but he can't. We advised him to read some brochures about the dangers of smoking.*

1 advise
2 help
3 warn (not to)
4 persuade
5 invite

3 Whose future?

Alan hopes to study computer science at university. What do you hope to do when you leave school?

a. On a piece of paper, write a short paragraph using some of the following verbs: **hope**, **would like**, **want**, **expect**, **prefer**. Remember to use **to** after the verbs. Do not write your name on the paper.

> ▷ *After school I would like to go to America for a year. My favourite hobby is playing tennis. I hope to be a professional tennis coach.*

b. A pupil collects the papers and gives them to other pupils. Take turns to read the paragraph you have been given to the class. If you think there is a mistake, correct it. Then try to guess who wrote it.

4 Alan's story

Answer the questions in full sentences. Say your answers.

> ▷ Why did Alan's mother want to buy him a computer?
> *She wanted to buy him a computer because he seemed to be very interested in them.*

1 Why didn't Alan's mother buy him a computer when he was ten?
2 When did his mother decide to give him a computer?
3 How long did she let him use it?
4 Why wouldn't she let him use it for longer?
5 What made Alan's mother realize that he was a computer addict?
6 What did she threaten to do?
7 What did Alan do that night?
8 What made him realize that the computer had become an obsession?
9 What does he hope to do next?
10 What would he like to do when he has finished studying?

5 Puzzle

Circle the verbs which take **to** + infinitive. Then use the circled words to solve the puzzle.

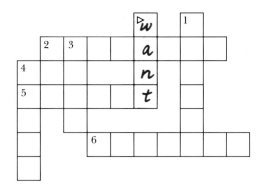

hope   threaten   refuse   enjoy
learn   avoid   dislike   pretend
expect   practise   want ✓   suggest

Down

> ▷ Why did Alan ___*want*___ to have a computer?
1 Why did he _____ to turn his computer off?
3 What did his mother _____ to do?
4 When did he _____ to use it?

Across

2 What did his mother _____ to do?
5 How did she _____ him to react?
6 Why did he _____ to be asleep?

6 Do you know what to do?

Mary and Rick don't know how to work the computer.

Complete what they say with a question word
(**how**, **where**, **which** etc.) + **to**, like this:

▷ RICK   I don't know *how to* turn it on.

1 RICK   Do you know _____ do first?

2 MARY   Yes, I do, but I'm not sure _____ put this disk.

3 RICK   I'd like to know _____ start this game.

4 MARY   There are so many keys. I don't know _____ press first.

5 RICK   We'll have to find out _____ make it start. Just press all the keys.

6 MARY   It's flashing! And it's making a funny noise! Do you know _____ turn it off?

7 RICK   No. Let's look at the book. Perhaps that will tell us _____ do.

8 MARY   I don't know _____ look at first. There are at least five computer books on the shelf.

7 Learning how to do it

a   Work with a partner.

One partner wants to learn to drive. The other partner is the driving instructor. It is the first driving lesson. Write a dialogue using **how to**, **when to**, **where to**, **which to** etc.

Useful words: engine, pedal, gear, brakes, indicator; accelerate, park, reverse, overtake.

▷ PARTNER A *I don't know what to do first.*
   PARTNER B *I'll show you how to start the engine.*

b   Together, read (or act) your dialogue to the class.

8 Where and why?

Work in two teams. Write the name of a place on pieces of paper. The place can be a country, a town, a street, a building, a shop or a room.

▷ *England, 10 Downing Street, the supermarket, the station, the kitchen, the White House.*

Fold your papers and put them in a pile.

Make two teams. A pupil from Team A takes a paper and opens it. The pupil must make a sentence with the word on the paper and **to**, saying why he/she went or is going to the place. There is a time limit of five seconds. Then it is Team B's turn. Score one point for each correct sentence.

▷ 10 Downing Street
  I'm going to 10 Downing Street to talk to the Prime Minister.

▷ the kitchen
  I'm going to the kitchen to wash the dishes.

42 Up and away

to + infinitive or **ing** form?
to + infinitive after adjectives and nouns

Dear Pam

I've just been staying with my cousin Kate in Egypt. We went to Luxor and I got the **chance to go up** in a hot air balloon! I didn't have **time to worry** about being scared. We just climbed into the basket, **impatient for the balloon to take off**.

As soon as we were in the air, Kate **started taking** photographs, but she soon **stopped to look** at the breathtaking view. I wanted to take photographs too, but I hadn't **remembered to take** my camera with me. It was **stupid of me to be** so careless.

We floated over the Nile. What a feeling! The view of the boats below us was **wonderful to watch**.

We left very early in the morning. There was a gentle wind at first, but after an hour the sun **started to shine**. At the end of our trip we **stopped looking** at the view and **began looking** for a safe **place to land.** People shouted and **waved** to us on the way down and tourists **stopped to watch** us landing. I was **happy to be** on the ground again, but it was a day I'll never forget.

Love   Christine

Grammar lesson

to + infinitive or ing form?

After some verbs we can use **to** + infinitive or an **ing** form without an important change in meaning. These verbs are **begin, continue, hate, like, love, start, intend, bother.**
> Kate *started to take/taking* photographs.

Remember that after **would like/love** only **to** + infinitive is possible.
> I *would like/love to go up* in a balloon.

After **stop, remember** and a few other verbs we can use **to** + infinitive or an **ing** form, but there is a change of meaning.
> She *stopped to look* at the view.
> (= She stopped in order to look. Purpose.)
> We stopped *looking* at the view.
> (= We didn't look any more.)
> I hadn't *remembered to take* it with me.
> (= I had forgotten to take . . .)
> I remembered *taking* it from my room.
> (= I remembered that I had taken . . .)

to + infinitive after adjectives and nouns

We use **to** + infinitive after many adjectives and nouns.

Adjective + (not) to
> I was **happy to be** on the ground again.

Other examples: **easy/difficult to**, **first/last to**, **glad/happy/pleased to**, **right/wrong to**, **safe/dangerous to**, **silly/foolish to**, **sorry to**.

Adjective + of/for + object + (not) to
> It was **stupid of me to be** so careless.
> I was **impatient for the balloon to take off**.

Noun + to
> We looked for a safe **place to land**.

Other examples: **plan/decision to**, **time/way to**.
Note also: **something/nothing to do**, **somewhere/nowhere to go** etc., **lots/a lot to do**.

1 A wonderful trip

a Write the correct form of the verb in brackets (). If two forms are possible, write both.

> Christine enjoys _visiting_ (visit) her cousin.

1 Kate likes _____ (do) exciting things.

2 She loves _____ (visit) new places.

3 Christine intended _____ (take) photographs of the river.

4 Unfortunately she didn't remember _____ (take) her camera.

5 Kate stopped _____ (take) photographs in order to enjoy the wonderful view.

6 After about an hour, the sun started _____ (shine).

7 When the balloon was landing, several people down below stopped _____ (watch).

8 People shouted and began _____ (wave) to the balloon.

9 Christine was happy _____ (be) on the ground.

10 Christine would like _____ (visit) Egypt again next year.

b Say five things that you remembered/didn't remember to do last week.

> I remembered to buy my friend a birthday present.
> I didn't remember to meet my sister on Tuesday.

c Say five things that you remember doing last year.

> I remember breaking my leg.
> I remember going camping in summer.

2 Things to do

Write what you think about the activities and places. Then take turns to read your sentences round the class.

> climbing without a rope
> Climbing without a rope is a silly/exciting/brave thing to do.
> museums
> Museums are interesting/fascinating/boring places to go to.

Activities	Places
climbing without a rope √	museums √
cleaning my room	supermarkets
reading about dinosaurs	caves
camping alone in the woods	a fair
writing letters	a market
picking up a poisonous snake	the beach
visiting other countries	a library
diving from a 10-metre board	a travel agency
speaking other languages	a haunted house
doing homework	a capital city

3 Wouldn't it be terrible?

a Make two teams. Each pupil in Team A writes a sentence beginning **It would be wonderful (not) to** . . . Each pupil in Team B writes a sentence beginning **It would be terrible (not) to** . . .

> TEAM A It would be wonderful to go up in a spaceship.
> TEAM B It would be terrible to fall out of a balloon.

b Pupils in Team A take turns to read out their sentences. Pupils in Team B must try to remember them. Pupils in Team B take turns to say a sentence which they remember. Score one point for each correctly remembered sentence.

Then play the game again with Team B's sentences. Which team can remember the most sentences?

It was Friday 13 January 1985. The Samsons had just moved into an old house in Borley in Essex.

The house, **built** about two hundred years earlier, had once belonged to a man **called** Boyson. Some people in the village said the house was **haunted**. They said that Boyson's daughter Mary had fallen in love with Harold, a blacksmith from the village. **Knowing** that her father would not allow them to marry, Mary had planned to run away with Harold. But her father, **having overheard** their plans, locked Mary in her room and shot Harold. When Mary found out, she hanged herself. Her father, **realizing** that he had done something terrible, died of a **broken** heart.

One night, John Samson was lying in bed **reading**. Suddenly he heard a strange **moaning** noise, like a man **crying**. Seconds later, the cigarette he was smoking went out and the room turned cold. Again, he thought he **heard** someone **crying** and **moving** about. **Having searched** all the rooms, he decided it must have been the wind. **Being** very tired, he fell asleep, with a lighted cigarette in his hand . . .

He dreamt that he could **hear** someone **knocking** loudly and that he could **smell** something **burning**. But it wasn't a dream. The bedroom curtains were on fire! Samson ran from the house.

Fifty people from the village gathered outside, **watching** the **burning** house. A policeman thought he saw a young woman **trapped** in an upstairs room, **knocking** at the window, but there was nobody in the house. Several people **saw** two figures **wearing** dark clothes **walking** through the flames. And an old man with a beard stood **crying** at the door . . .

No bodies were found in the ruins. No one was **surprised**.

---

haunted having a ghost living there

moaning low, sad, crying sound

blacksmith person who makes shoes for horses

trapped unable to get out

Grammar lesson

Participles as adjectives

We use present participles and past participles as adjectives.

> a **burning** house   a **haunted** house
> a **moaning** noise   a **broken** heart

Learn the following pairs of participle adjectives and study how they are used.

amazing	amazed
amusing	amused
annoying	annoyed
boring	bored
confusing	confused
disappointing	disappointed
exciting	excited
fascinating	fascinated
frightening	frightened
interesting	interested
relaxing	relaxed
satisfying	satisfied
surprising	surprised
tiring	tired
worrying	worried

*The story was **boring**. We were **bored**.*
*The end was **frightening**. I felt **frightened**.*
*It was an **interesting** story. I was **interested**.*

Participles instead of clauses

We also use participles to shorten a relative clause.

> two figures **wearing** dark clothes
> (= figures who were wearing dark clothes)
> a house **built** two hundred years earlier
> (= which had been built two hundred years earlier)

We use participles in this way when two actions happen at the same time:

> *He was lying in bed **reading**.*
> (He was lying in bed and he was reading.)

after the verbs **sit**, **stand**, **lie** and **come**:

> *An old man **stood crying**.*

after the verbs **see**, **watch**, **notice**, **feel**, **hear**, **listen to**, **smell** + object:

> *He **heard** someone **crying**.*
> *He **smelt** something **burning**.*

In written language more than in spoken language, a participle is often used instead of a clause with **because**, **since** or **as** to give a reason for something:

> ***Knowing** that her father would not allow them to marry, Mary . . .*
> (Because she knew that her father . . .)
> ***Being** very tired, he fell asleep.*
> (As he was very tired, he fell asleep.)

instead of a time clause with **when**, **after**, **before** or **while**:

> ***Realizing** that he had done something terrible, Boyson died of a broken heart.*
> (When he realized that he had done . . .)

to show that one action happens after another, with **having** + past participle:

> ***Having searched** all the rooms, he decided it must be the wind.*
> (After/When he had searched all the rooms . . .)

1 Who was it?

Say the sentences using a participle instead of a relative clause.

> ▷ The story which has been told in Borley for over a hundred years is true.
> *The story told in Borley for over a hundred years is true.*

1 The old house which had been built two hundred years earlier had once belonged to Boyson.
2 John Samson heard the noise of a man who was crying.
3 The woman who was seen at the window was the ghost of Mary Boyson.
4 The strange moaning noise which had been heard by John Samson on the night of the fire was Boyson's ghost crying.
5 The two figures who were wearing dark clothes were the ghosts of Mary Boyson and Harold.
6 The old man who was standing at the door crying was the ghost of Mary's father.

2 Ghostly happenings

Make one sentence using a participle, without changing the meaning. Write your answers.

> ▷ The ghosts appeared and disappeared. They left no trace.
> *The ghosts appeared and disappeared, leaving no trace.*

1 The Samsons arrived in Borley.
   They knew nothing about the ghosts.
2 Mr Samson ran out of the burning house.
   He shouted loudly.
3 Some neighbours came.
   They were carrying buckets.
4 The villagers gathered.
   They watched the fire.
5 Three firemen arrived.
   They brought fire equipment.
6 A young woman was standing at the window.
   She was knocking at the window.
7 An old man was standing in the door.
   He was crying.
8 The Samsons moved to London.
   They left behind a ruined house.

3 I'm not frightened!

Cross out the wrong adjective.

JENNY I'm ▷ boring/bored . What shall we do?

NICK I'll tell you a good ghost story. Is anybody

¹ frightened/frightening of ghosts?

BEN Of course not. I'm ² fascinating/ fascinated by ghost

stories. Jane's ³ interesting/interested in them, too. I'd

love to see a real ghost.

NICK I think everybody likes a good ghost story. But I don't think it

would be very ⁴ amusing/amused to see a ghost. I'd be

⁵ terrifying/terrified .

BEN But just think how ⁶ exciting/excited it would be. And

what an ⁷ amazing/ amazed story I could tell at school.

Just imagine how ⁸ surprising/surprised everyone would

be to hear a story of a headless ghost running around Merton

in chains . . .

JENNY Well, you'll be ⁹ disappointing/ disappointed , Ben.

There aren't any ghosts in Merton, I'm afraid.

BEN Who says there are no ghosts in Merton? I even think that our

house is haunted. Some ¹⁰ worrying/worried things have

happened. For example, yesterday four plates fell on the

floor and broke.

JENNY But Ben, that wasn't a ghost. You were washing up.

4 What happened?

Rewrite the sentences using a participle, without changing the meaning. Remember to use **having** + past participle when necessary.

▷ John Samson bought the old house in Borley because he didn't know about the ghosts.
John Samson bought the old house in Borley, not knowing about the ghosts.

▷ Because she had fallen in love with Harold, Mary wanted to marry him.
Having fallen in love with Harold, Mary wanted to marry him.

1 Because she knew that her father would not allow her to marry Harold, Mary planned to run away.

2 Because he had overheard their plans, Boyson locked Mary in her room.

3 After she had found out the truth, Mary hanged herself.

4 When he found his daughter dead, Boyson realized he had done a terrible thing.

5 Because he heard a strange noise, Samson looked to see what it was.

6 After he had searched all the rooms, he went back into the bedroom.

7 Because he didn't find anything, he got into bed again.

8 As he was very tired, he soon fell asleep.

9 Because he had forgotten to put out his cigarette, he started a fire.

10 Since it was made of wood, the old house was soon burnt to the ground.

5 I've seen a ghost!

Some people say they have seen a ghost. What did they see, feel, hear etc.? Say your answers in a sentence with an **ing** form.

▷ MOLLY   I saw a white figure. It moved silently up the stairs.
Molly saw a white figure moving silently up the stairs.

JOE   I heard a woman's voice. It called my name, quite clearly.

TED   I felt a cold wind. It blew through the closed door of my room. I saw a dark shadow. It passed through the bedroom wall.

BILL   In the cellar I saw a pale yellow ball of light. It moved around silently.

TOM   I was having dinner in the dining-room. There was another guest. He was wearing old-fashioned clothes.

HILDA   I was looking round a graveyard. Suddenly I felt a cold hand. It touched my cheek.

MARTHA   I heard a child. It was shouting for help. There were no children anywhere.

6 Write a ghost story

Invent a ghost story. Say where you were and what you saw, felt, noticed or heard.

Write a short paragraph similar to the ones in Exercise 5. Read your story to the class and vote for the most mysterious or most imaginative one.

7 The haunted house

Play the game like this. Make your sentences as funny as you wish. Remember to use an **ing** form.

PUPIL A   *In the haunted house there was a ghost playing the piano.*

PUPIL B   *In the haunted house there was a ghost playing the piano and a candle floating through the air.*

PUPIL C   *In the haunted house there was a ghost playing the piano, a candle floating through the air and a skeleton in chains smoking a pipe.*

Continue. How many things can you remember in the right order?

It was New Year's Eve, 1880. Karl Benz and his wife Berta were trying very hard to start his new engine. **Although** they had worked hard for hours, they could not get it to go. Karl had just built the first motor car engine in the world, but it wouldn't start.

Berta refused to give in, **because** she had a strong will. She believed in her husband's ability, **so** she always supported him. Even **before** they were married, she had given him money **so that** he could afford to try out his ideas.

Berta persuaded Karl to try again and again and not stop **until** he succeeded. And then, a few seconds before midnight, the miracle happened. The engine suddenly burst into life. The bells rang out to welcome the New Year, **while** the engine hissed and banged. What a wonderful noise!

Grammar lesson

Link words

Link words (**when, because, so** etc.) introduce a subordinate clause. The word order in a subordinate clause is the same as the word order in a main clause: subject, verb, object.

Words such as **when, while, as, before, after, until** and **as soon as** can introduce a *time* clause.

> Even **before** they were married, she had given him money.
> Berta persuaded Karl to try **until** he succeeded.

In time clauses we often use past or perfect tenses, but not future tenses (not **will** or **would**).

We use **although, though** and **even though** to introduce a *contrast*.

> **Although** they had worked for hours, they could not get it to go.

We use **because, since** and **as** to introduce *reason* and **so** for *result*.

> Berta refused to give in, **because** she had a strong will.
> She believed in her husband's ability, **so** she always supported him.

We use **so that** or **in order that** to introduce *purpose*.

> Berta gave Karl money, **so that** he could afford to try out his ideas.

1 The first woman driver

Read the story of Berta Benz's first journey by car. Cross out the wrong words.

Eight years later, Benz had developed a vehicle to go with the engine, but ▷ before/~~when~~ he could show it to the public, someone had to drive it. Berta believed in the car, 1 so/although she decided to drive it first, before her husband. 2 Because/So she wanted to keep her plan secret, Berta told Karl that she and their two young sons were going to visit their grandmother. She didn't say how they were going to get there. They set off 3 before/until it grew light, 4 so that/while Karl wouldn't see them. 5 So/Although Berta didn't know how to steer, she managed to keep the car on the road. 6 When/Until they reached a village, they filled up with water. Then, a little further on, the vehicle suddenly stopped 7 so that/because the tank was empty. Richard remembered that his father had once bought a cleaning fluid from a chemist's, 8 so that/so they pushed the car to the next town. 9 After/Until they had left Heidelberg, the car stopped again, 10 so/because the fuel pipe was blocked with dust from the roads. 11 While/Before the two sons were discussing what to do, Berta took a long hair pin and pushed it up the pipe. She was determined to reach Pforzheim. 12 As/Although the noisy car with its three tired passengers finally arrived, Berta knew that she and her husband had shown the world how the cars of the future would look.

2 How 'Model T' was born

Read the story of Henry Ford. Put in suitable link words. Sometimes, more than one answer is possible.

▷ _When_ Ford had driven his first car over a thousand miles, he sold it. 1 _____ he wanted to improve his work, he used the money to build two other bigger cars. He didn't go into the car business until 1899, 2 _____ he founded his own company. His dream was to build light cars which were strong but also cheap, 3 _____ everyone could buy them. Ford introduced the Model A in 1903, but it wasn't 4 _____ he built the Model T in 1908 that his great success began. The car was nicknamed 'Tin Lizzie' and sold for $825. Just six months 5 _____ 'Tin Lizzie' had been built, Ford was selling a hundred cars a day. Lizzie wasn't beautiful, but she was cheap and reliable. 6 _____ Lizzie was black, Ford told his customers, 'You can have any colour you like, as long as it's black.'

3 Inventors

Work with a partner. Write a story about the life of a famous inventor. Use: **when, after, before, while, until, because, so, (in order) to.** Your story does not have to be true. Write about his/her life, what he/she invented and why.

▷ _Our inventor is Harry Rogers. He hated having to run a bath, so he decided to invent a machine to do it for him . . ._

Take turns to read your stories to the class.

steer turn the wheel of a vehicle to make it go left or right

hair pin

45 Trig's top ten tips
Verbs with adverbs and prepositions;
Verbs with two objects

'Good evening, Earthlings! I have a very important **message to give to you** from my friends on Planet Triglon. The message is: '**Give Planet Earth a chance!**' We have been watching you for hundreds of years. You are not looking after yourselves or your planet. We want to help you, so we have **worked out** a few ways for you to **cut down on** pollution and to **look after** your health. Please **look at** the information sheets that my assistant will **hand out**. I have **made** a list of ideas **for you**. When you have read it, I would like you to **think of** some ideas of your own.'

Trig's top ten tips

1   **Pick up** rubbish
2   **Switch** all lights **off** at night
3   **Ask for** ozone-friendly aerosols
4   **Look out for** recyclable goods
5   Don't **cut** your trees **down**
6   **Think of** new ways to keep fit
7   **Cut down on** unhealthy food
8   **Take up** a sport
9   **Do without** sweets and fizzy drinks
10 **Give up** smoking

tip a piece of advice

Grammar lesson

Verbs with adverbs and prepositions

Phrasal verbs

These are formed with a verb + adverb, such as **give up**. Sometimes the meaning is clear, but often the two words together have a special meaning which we cannot guess. For example, **give up** means 'stop (doing) something'.

> *Give up smoking.*

Here are some more examples:

> **turn** something **down** (refuse something)
> **put** something **off** (postpone something)
> **ring** someone **up** (telephone someone)

Some phrasal verbs do not have an object (**sit down**, **stand up**, **go away**). Others do (**cut something down**). If the object is a noun, it can come before or after the adverb.

> *Don't **cut** your trees **down**.*
> *Don't **cut down** your trees.*

But if the object is a pronoun (him, her, it, them) it must come between the verb and the adverb.

> *Don't **cut** them **down**.*

Here are some more examples:

> **switch** something **on/off**
> **turn** something **down/up/on/off**
> **put** something **on/off**
> **give** something **away**

Prepositional verbs

These are formed with a verb + preposition + object, for example **look for** something, **do without** something. The preposition always goes before the object.

> ***Think of** new ways to keep fit.*
> ***Do without** sweets and fizzy drinks.*

Here are some more examples:

> **ask for**, **agree with**, **care about**, **decide on**, **look after**, **look at**, **pay for**, **wait for**

Phrasal prepositional verbs

These are formed with a verb + adverb + preposition + object, for example **cut down on** something, **look out for** something/someone. The word order does not change.

> ***Look out for** recyclable goods.*
> ***Cut down on** unhealthy food.*

Verbs with two objects

Some verbs such as **give** can have two objects, a direct object and an indirect object.

When the direct object (the thing) is more important, we use this word order.

> *Subject   Verb   Indirect object   Direct object*
> Trig   gave   the Earthlings   a message.

When the indirect object (the person) is more important, we use the following order.

> *Subject   Verb   Direct object   Indirect object*
> Trig   gave   a message   to the Earthlings.

Other verbs with two objects are **offer**, **pass**, **send**, **show**, **teach**, **write**; **buy**, **make**. With **buy** and **make** we use **for** instead of **to**.

> *Trig **made them** a list of top ten tips.* OR
> *Trig **made** a list of top ten tips **for them**.*

1   More tips

a   Help Trig to add some more tips to his list. Write five sentences using some of the following phrases: **clear up**, **take up**, **give up**, **turn on/off**, **look for**, **look after**, **pick up**, **cut down**, like this:

> ▷   *Give up eating crisps and drinking cola.*
> ▷   *Look after animals and plants.*

b   Take turns to read your sentences round the class.

2 Rubbish!

a Make a list of ten things which you and your family throw away every day. Say the sentences round the class.

> ▷ *I throw sweet wrappers away.*
> ▷ *My parents throw old newspapers away.*

b Take turns to ask and answer questions round the class, like this:

> ▷ PUPIL A *Do you throw a lot of paper away?*
> PUPIL B *Yes, I do throw quite a lot of it away.* OR
> *No, I don't throw it away. I recycle it.*

3 Giving up

a Which of the following things could you easily give up? Which couldn't you give up?

sweets   crisps
chocolate   ice-cream
chewing gum   fizzy drinks
biscuits   chips

> ▷ *I could easily give up sweets.*
> *I couldn't give up crisps very easily.*

Just one more,
then I'll give up ice-creams.

b Think about the things your family and friends do or eat. Write a list of things you think they should give up. Take turns to read them round the class.

> ▷ *My uncle smokes and he doesn't take enough exercise. I think he ought to give up smoking and take up jogging.*

4 Questionnaire

Answer the questions below. Write two sentences for each question. Use a pronoun object (**it** or **them**), like this:

> ▷ What do you do with glass bottles? (throw away/recycle)
> *I throw them away.*
> *I don't recycle them.*

1 What happens to drinks cans and plastic bottles in your house? (throw away/recycle)

_____

_____

2 You go into the kitchen to get a glass of water. It is getting dark, but it is still possible to see. (leave on/turn off)

_____

_____

3 You are in the park with some small children. They do not know what to do with their empty crisp packets. What do you tell them to do? (leave behind/take away)

_____

_____

4 You go into the living room. The television is on but no one is watching it. (switch off/leave on)

_____

_____

5 You're alone at home. The tap in the kitchen has been left on. (turn off/leave on)

_____

_____

5 Fit and healthy

Look at the pictures below. Nick is very worried about his friend Sam. Sam is very unfit but he wants to take part in the school marathon. Nick has been trying to help Sam improve his health. Say two sentences about each picture. Use the words given, like this:

▷ *Nick sent Sam a health and fitness magazine.*
Nick sent a health and fitness magazine to Sam.

Nick/send/Sam

Nick/lend/Sam

Nick/buy/Sam

Nick/make/Sam

Nick/lend/Sam

Nick/send/Sam

Nick/buy/Sam

Nick/buy/Sam

Nick/lend/Sam

6 Team tips

Make two teams. How many different ways can you think of to cut down on pollution and make people healthier? Write as many sentences as you can. Use the phrases on page 147. Score one point for each correct sentence.

▷ *We could try to make people give up smoking.*
We could encourage people to turn off lights they aren't using.

Acknowledgements

Oxford University Press
Walton Street, Oxford OX2 6DP

Oxford New York
Athens Auckland Bangkok Bombay
Calcutta Cape Town Dar es Salaam Delhi
Florence Hong Kong Istanbul Karachi
Kuala Lumpur Madras Madrid Melbourne
Mexico City Nairobi Paris Singapore
Taipei Tokyo Toronto

and associated companies in
Berlin Ibadan

OXFORD and OXFORD ENGLISH
are trade marks of Oxford University Press.

ISBN 0 19 431364 6
ISBN 0 19 431357 3 (Greek edition)

© Oxford University Press 1994

First published 1994
Second impression 1995

No unauthorized photocopying

Paintings by Heather Clarke

Typeset in Baskerville and Frutiger by
Pentacor PLC

Printed in Spain

The Publisher and Author would like to thank the
following for their kind permission to use extracts
and adaptations from copyright material:

Care for the Wild: pp. 108–113.
Cornish Seal Sanctuary: p. 114.
Dorling Kindersley Children's Books: p. 42, text
    adapted from *Children's Illustrated Encyclopedia*.
Kogan Page Limited: p. 34, puzzle from *Test Your
    Own Aptitude*, 1st edition, by Barrett & Williams,
    1980.
Oxford University Press: pp. 25, 26, 44, 121, 145,
    text adapted from *Oxford Children's Encyclopedia*.
Sphere Books Ltd: pp. 32, 34, puzzles from *Junior
    Mensa Puzzle Book* by Russell & Carter, 1989.
The Guardian: p. 88, adapted from 'Bright Spark',
    article by Kate Murphy in *Guardian Source Book*.

The Publisher and Author would like to thank the
following for their permission to reproduce
pictures:

Allsport (UK) Ltd: cover, Cole (balloon); cover
    & p. 63, Giani (Patissier climbing); p. 64, Klein
    (parachutes); p. 138, Mao (balloons).
Aquarius Library: p. 16 (Macaulay Culkin, star of
    'Home Alone').
Ardea London Ltd: p. 116, Gohier (killer whale);
    p. 118 (aye-aye).
Bridgeman Art Library: p. 44, Christie's, London
    (portrait of Master Day); p. 128, Goya (Blind
    Man's Bluff, detail).
Bruce Coleman Ltd: p. 40, Burton (*Coelurus*
    chasing pterosaur); p. 108, Murray (green
    turtle); p. 118, Wothe (aye-aye).
Comstock: p. 21 (Macchu Picchu).
Mary Evans Picture Library: p. 8, Galaxy Search
    (UFO); p. 13, Molino (Loch Ness monster);
    p. 15, Mangur (kraken); p. 84 (Joshua Slocum);
    p. 84, Randall (Slocum's boat, 'Spray'); cover,
    Magnus (sea serpent, adapted).
Fortean Picture Library: p. 15, Magnus
    (sea monster, adapted).
Robert Harding Picture Library: p. 110, Hart
    (beach).
The Hutchison Library: p. 24, Woodhead
    (Ethiopians watching television).
The Image Bank: p. 4, Newman (sheep); p. 5,
    Rokeach (farm building in Australia); p. 20,
    Hamilton (sunset); p. 60, Smith (white-water
    rafting); pp. 78, 79, Edmunds (Easter Island
    statues); p. 81, Gordon (Easter Island statue);
    p. 81, Miller (Easter Island statues); p. 82,
    Meola (sea); cover & p. 90, Block (orang-utan
    with baby).
The Mansell Collection Ltd: pp. 47, 130 (the
    Shepherd's Calendar).
The National Trust Photographic Library: p. 44,
    Burton (the Hardwick portrait).
NHPA: p. 20, Kraseman (British Columbia); p. 21
    (Tierra del Fuego); p. 30, Dalton (vampire
    bat); p. 30, Heuclin (pit viper); p. 30,
    Cambridge (wolf spider); p. 92, Gainsburgh
    (tropical rainforest); p. 109, Aitkin (turtle
    laying eggs); p. 117, Carne Molla (humpback
    whale).
Oxford Scientific Films Ltd Photo Library: p. 117,
    Hall (sand tiger shark).
Oxford University Press: p. 30, *The Life of
    Vertebrates*, 2nd edition, by Young, 1962
    (*Varanus* lizard); p. 31, *ibid.* (*Gecko*, adapted).
Planet Earth Pictures/Seaphot Ltd: p. 111, Bell
    (loggerhead turtle); cover & p. 114, Merdsoy
    (seal pup); p. 116, Perrine (spotted dolphins);
    p. 117, Salm (sea lion).

Rex Features Ltd: p. 86, Jorgensen (Live Aid
    concert).
Science Photo Library Ltd: p. 20, Earth Satellite
    Corporation (American continent).
Tony Stone Images: p. 21 (Peruvian people);
    p. 31, Ulrich (chameleon); p. 56, Pobereskin
    (Park Avenue, New York); p. 57, Ortner
    (Manhattan skyline); p. 60, McKelvie (bungy
    jumper); p. 84, Berger (waves); p. 100,
    Brettnacher (sunset); p. 134 (electronic
    circuit); p. 137, Johnson (organic geometry).
The Telegraph Colour Library Ltd: p. 20 (Golden
    Gate bridge); p. 21, Tamborrino (Acapulco);
    p. 34, Benelux (students taking exam); p. 34,
    Hallinan (woman winning race); p. 59 (Louvre
    pyramid, Paris); p. 59, Liard (Prague); cover &
    p. 60 (windsurfer); p. 117 (emperor penguins);
    cover & p. 146 (abstract picture of earth).
Bob Thomas Sports Photography: p. 60,
    Wiesmeier (Glowacz climbing).

There are drawings by Richard Allen (front cover),
Stephen Hibberd (rat & *Gecko*, p. 31)
and Witless Latherum (pp. 30, 31, 126).

Every effort has been made to trace the owners
of copyright material used in this book, but we
should be pleased to hear from any copyright
holder whom we have been unable to contact.